A Touch of Cleveland History

Stories from the First 200 Years

BOB RICH

GRAY & COMPANY, PUBLISHERS

CLEVELAND

To my true love, Joan

These stories were originally published as a weekly newspaper series in The Plain Dealer.

Photos credited as "CSU" are from the Cleveland Press Collection, Cleveland State University Archives.

Gray & Company, Publishers
www.grayco.com

ISBN 978-1-938441-33-2
Printed in the United States of America
v2

Contents

A Touch of Cleveland History

Indian Clashes Preceded Cleaveland Expedition

Cleveland's history starts with Moses Cleaveland arriving here July 22, 1796, but it actually goes back to 1787, the year that the Confederation Congress established the Northwest Territory, covering what would eventually become Ohio, Illinois, Indiana, Michigan, Wisconsin, and part of Minnesota.

Some provisions of the Northwest Ordinance guaranteed rights that anticipated the Bill of Rights, encouraged public education and forbade slavery north of the Ohio River.

The ordinance respected land held by Indians, but the dirt-poor, ragged squatters who swarmed onto the land didn't care about land titles or Indian rights. Settlers would chop out a clearing in the forest and plant their seeds. If the territorial government sent troops to burn them out they came back—or others did.

Alexander Hamilton and the Federalist party wanted to sell the land to settlers to pay off the Revolutionary War debt, but Thomas Jefferson saw public lands as an opportunity to find independence. "Whenever there is in any country uncultivated lands and unemployed poor, it is clear that the laws of property have been so far extended as to violate natural right." Asserting that needy settlers shouldn't be made to pay the war debt, he predicted: "They will settle the lands in spite of everybody."

He was right—the settlers kept pouring in illegally, without benefit of land titles, and the Indian tribes reacted with savage attacks that led to massacres by the settlers. The frontier was aflame from Ohio to Louisiana, with the tribes egged on and armed by the British in Detroit and the Spanish in New Orleans.

Frontier states threatened to secede unless the national government could protect them.

President Washington tried. Two poorly trained armies were sent out. The first in 1789 was ambushed near Fort Wayne, Ind., and in 1790, a 2,700-man army was almost destroyed near Fort Recovery, Ohio, by Little Turtle and his Miamis and Shawnees.

Anthony Wayne came to an agreement with Native
Americans to secure a large portion of land for the
Connecticut Land Co. *(Cleveland Public Library)*

Washington then placed Revolutionary War general "Mad
Anthony" Wayne in command of the western troops. Tough, hard-
drinking and in constant pain from gout, he hammered discipline
into his troops for 18 months, then marched north from Fort Washington, near Cincinnati, building a line of forts to protect his sup-
plies; the names of these forts survive in small Ohio towns such as
Fort Recovery, Defiance, Jefferson, and Greenville.

The British, fearing Wayne would attack Fort Detroit, sent
troops to build their own fort, Miami, on the Maumee River, site
of present-day Maumee, Ohio. Aug. 24, 1794, Wayne found Indians
under Tecumseh, Blue Jacket and Little Turtle, hiding behind fallen
trees.

"Charge the damn rascals with the bayonet!" Wayne said when
the Indians fired. When the warriors fled to Fort Miami, where they

had been promised protection, the British shut the gates rather than risk another war.

Wayne and the Indians signed a treaty at Fort Greenville in June 1795. Connecticut had once claimed a big part of the Ohio country. But now the lands 60 miles west of the Cuyahoga River and south for 40 miles were given to the Indians, and the land east of the river up to the Pennsylvania line was confirmed as belonging to Connecticut—its Western Reserve.

Within weeks Connecticut investors formed a real estate venture, the Connecticut Land Co., and bought all 3 million acres for $1,200,000. In May 1796, they sent their chief surveyor and one of their biggest investors, General Moses Cleaveland, to lay out a town and lots at the Cuyahoga's mouth.

The general took his 50-man party through New York state, and at Canandaigua he parleyed with Iroquois tribes to, as he quaintly put it, "extinguish" remaining claims they might feel they had to the Western Reserve.

After four days of feasting, dancing and drinking, the Indians accepted 500 New York State dollars, two cows and more "red-eye" to stay peaceful.

July 4th, the surveying party passed the Pennsylvania state boundary marker and found itself in the Western Reserve, at Conneaut, which they christened Port Independence.

That night there was much firing of rifle salutes to the American Federation, to the president, to the land company; and the bottle was passed around for many more toasts until the men fell asleep in the middle of the wilderness.

In the morning the men would start their journey to the mouth of the Cuyahoga River to lay out their capital for New Connecticut.

Moses Finds the Promised Land

July 5th, 1796, after a merry (and liquid) Fourth of July the night
before, Moses Cleaveland and his 50-man surveying crew from the
Connecticut Land Co. set out from Conneaut to find the mouth
of the Cuyahoga River, where they would lay out a new capital for
their Promised Land.

Cleaveland was a burly, powerful-looking man with a swarthy
complexion that may have fooled Indians into thinking he was one
of them. He was a Yale graduate with experience in the Revolutionary War and had practiced law for 30 years in his hometown of
Canterbury, Conn.

He was appointed general of militia by the state. Cleaveland was
the logical man to head the survey of the company's newly acquired
3 million acres east of the Cuyahoga River; plus, his own money
was at stake.

Real estate speculation was the way to get rich (or get swindled)
in those early days of the American republic. The Connecticut investors had paid 40 cents an acre for their Western Reserve holdings, and the chances of getting rich looked very good. New England
was filled with landless, unemployed men who would be able to lay
down a little cash for their own lot.

And so Cleaveland's surveying party of axmen, chainmen,
rodmen and compassmen hacked its way through a trackless forest,
laying out 5-mile square townships, sometimes eating boiled rattlesnake and berries when hunters came back empty-handed. With
a broiling sun, mosquitoes, swamps and rainstorms, most of the
party suffered from dysentery, cramps and fevers—and they had 55
miles to go from the Pennsylvania border to the Cuyahoga.

Somewhere along the line, Moses Cleaveland and some of his
men got into a boat and coasted along Lake Erie until July 22, 1796,
when they headed into the mouth of the sand-choked Cuyahoga—
"crooked river," in the Iroquois language.

Now they met the real enemy: swarms of malarial mosquitoes
that rose to attack the sweaty bargemen. Above the eastern bank of

Moses Cleaveland led a team that surveyed what would become Cleveland, Ohio. *(Cleveland Public Library)*

the river, the heights were covered with chestnut, oak, walnut and maple trees, but down in the valley, they could smell the swamps and the decay; because the river had so many sandbars, a large sailing vessel would never make it from the lake into the river.

But no matter—the sandbars could be dredged. Here was a river from the interior of Ohio feeding into a freshwater lake, a river that would carry product out and finished goods in. This was the place to establish the capital of New Connecticut.

So the Cleaveland party landed at the foot of today's St. Clair Ave., climbed up the hill and set to work surveying town lots. The men took 10 acres in the center of the plateau to establish a New England village-style Public Square; pushed a north-south street that they called Ontario through the center, and an even wider path from east-to-west called Superior.

After three months of surveying, Cleaveland took his crew back home to Connecticut.

Cleaveland never came back, but his surveying crew had complimented him by naming the settlement after him. Years later he said, "While I was in New Connecticut I laid out a town on the bank of Lake Erie, which was called by my name, and I believe the child is now born who may live to see that place as large as Old Windham." Since Old Windham's population was 2,200, eventually, he was proved right.

Only three people from the Cleaveland party chose to stay: Job Stiles, his wife, Tabitha, and Joseph Landon, and they shared a log cabin put up by the surveyors on what is now W. 6th St. and Superior. Their only company was a little group of Seneca Indians nearby. To the east and south was unbroken wilderness filled with wild game—turkey, bear, deer and timber wolves; west was the river and millions of trees; north was drinking-water pure Lake Erie.

Landon got one blast of winter winds whistling off the lake, and Cleaveland's population dropped by one-third.

It got right back up there when Edward Paine arrived and began to trade with the Chippewa and Ottawa Indians. He would pull up stakes several years later and found Painesville.

That winter, the Indians befriended their white neighbors in the cabin on the hill, supplying them with game. Eventually, they would lose their ancestral lands to these same neighbors for a little money and a lot of whiskey.

Whoever nastily nicknamed Cleveland "The Mistake on the Lake" must have been there that first year when a few pioneers straggled in in the spring, in time to catch the ague (malaria) with chills and fever. When they recovered, they left for higher ground 6 miles southeast in what became Newburg, or east to Doan's Corners (now E. 105th and Euclid).

By 1800, the total population was one family. You wouldn't have wanted to bet on Cleveland's survival much less its growth to the size of Old Windham, Conn.—unless, that is, you knew that one family in that one cabin belonged to Lorenzo Carter.

Log Cabin Hero

Carter Held Settlement

In the spring of 1797, a remarkable man named Lorenzo Carter brought his family from Vermont to the tiny pioneer settlement of Cleveland. Founder Moses Cleaveland had taken his surveying crew from the Connecticut Land Co. back home in October the year before and would never return to his namesake village. It would be up to Carter and a few others whether Cleveland survived into the turn of the century.

Carter, 6 feet tall, was considered a giant. He had a swarthy complexion and black hair that hung down to his shoulders; also, a reputation for hunting, tracking, shooting and being very good with his fists—and quick to use them.

Lorenzo Carter and family would stay on the bank of the Cuyahoga River when others that straggled in during the next few years left the swampy, malarial-ridden area for higher, healthier grounds.

On paper, Cleveland, with its river from the interior to Lake Erie, should have been the ideal distribution point for the whole Western Reserve, but the river just barely flowed into the lake, choked by silt and sand of the harbor. Even Carter's brother-in-law couldn't take the malarial shakes and chills and left. Until April 1800, the Carters were the only white family left in Cleveland town.

Lorenzo Carter built a large log cabin, with two rooms and a spacious garret, and started a ferry at the foot of Superior St. When the Indians came to his cabin "under the hill" with their furs to trade, he had goods such as calico and trinkets for the women and he had what the braves wanted most—whiskey.

People used to say that he was all the law that Cleveland had, and he was soon appointed a constable and later a major of militia by the territorial governor.

As the stories go, any tough who rode into this little frontier clearing felt compelled to try himself out bare-knuckled, against Carter. And the major never lost.

Lorenzo Carter made his home on the east bank of the Cuyahoga River. *(CSU)*

One day, he returned from a hunt to find that a party of thirsty Indians had broken into his warehouse and gotten into the whiskey barrel. Carter exploded, slapped the drunks around, kicked several into the swamps, and promptly forgot about the incident. The braves didn't. Two of their best marksmen ambushed him in the woods, took their shots and missed. The major didn't.

After that, the Indians figured he was immortal and often called on him to judge their tribal feuds. He spoke several of their dialects.

He wasn't admired by everybody. Solid New England Yankees didn't like the riffraff that hung out at his cabin saloon. One prominent early settler, lawyer Samuel Huntington, wrote back to Moses Cleaveland in 1802 that Carter "gathers about him all the itinerant Vagabonds that he meets with, out of whom he gets all his labour done for their board and Whiskey; over whom he has an absolute control—organizing a phalanx of Desperadoes and setting all Laws at defiance." And there was perhaps some jealousy involved at his cornering the Indian fur trade.

And yet it was Carter, with his rifle and dogs, who, when every member of the tiny village was down with malarial fever and chills, brought in the wild game to feed them.

He was no civil libertarian, but he didn't like slavery. When a canoe upset in Lake Erie in the spring of 1806, drowning a white family in the frigid water, the only survivor was a black man, Ben, who was cared for at Carter's cabin until the fall when two Kentuckians rode in and claimed that he had been their slave.

Carter told Ben that he didn't have to go back to Kentucky, but Ben talked to his former masters and agreed to go back with them. By the time the small party got to Newburgh, two of Carter's friends appeared with rifles. "Ben, you damned fool, jump off that horse and take to the woods!" said one. Ben jumped, made it to the woods and presumably to Canada and freedom; the Kentuckians ran the other way.

With all the mixed feelings about Lorenzo Carter, his spacious cabin was the social center, schoolhouse, jail and inn for an area that by 1810 had grown to only 300 people in the entire township. When 16 of Cleveland's 18 families formed a lending library in 1811, Carter kept Goldsmith's "History of Greece" and "Don Quixote" out so long that he had to pay a dollar apiece in fines. Apparently, there was a touch of intellect to the man of action.

Movies and books continue to pour out endless Daniel Boone and Wyatt Earp stories. Yet in Cleveland, was just such a frontiersman and adventurer—a man who left his enduring mark on a struggling community by surviving and showing others how to survive.

There's no statue of Lorenzo Carter in Public Square to go with founder Moses Cleaveland's; just a fading name on a building, the Pick-Carter Hotel.

But he was the first of the remarkable men and women who would force-feed the new, infant village into the brawling giant it became many years later.

Frontier Era Ends as East, West Sides Start to Grow

Ohio became the 17th state in 1803 and prepared for the swarms of settlers its new status would bring, but little Cleveland town couldn't seem to get off the ground.

Recent prominent arrivals like Samuel Huntington, a lawyer and nephew of a signer of the Declaration of Independence, escaped Cleveland's malarial swamps for busy Newburgh, 6 miles down the Cuyahoga to the southeast. Newburgh looked like it was going to be the great metropolitan center, the capital of the Western Reserve.

Then, a much more serious threat arose from the west side of the Cuyahoga. Companies that owned land there decided "a time had come for the formal and final extinguishment of the remaining Indian claims." Moses Cleaveland's Connecticut Land Co. and the owners of the Firelands—(today's Erie and Huron counties)—which had been set aside for Connecticut Revolutionary War veterans who had been burnt out by British raiders—were able to get the federal government to arrange a council with the Western Reserve Indian tribes, and some of the New York state Indians who still claimed some rights to their lands.

This was to take place in Cleveland on June 5, 1805, but the Western Indians didn't show up. The treaty commissioners eventually met with the tribes, possibly near Sandusky—Wyandots, Ottawas, Chippewas, Munsees, Delawares, Shawnees, Senecas and Pottowattomies. After much giving of trinkets, calico, and liberal applications of that great pacifier, Monongahela rye whiskey, a treaty was signed with the Indians on the Fourth of July—Independence Day for the American commissioners—the end of independence for these American Indians.

Commissioner William Deane outlined it in a letter: "On the 4th instant, we closed a treaty with the Indians, for the unextinguished part of the Connecticut Reserve, and on account of the United States. . . . Mr. Phelps and myself pay about $7,000 in cash, and about $12,000 in six yearly payments . . . government pays $13,760, that is the annual interest, to the tribes . . . forever. The expense of the treaty will be about $5,000, including rum, tobacco, bread, meat, presents."

Another writer of that period said, "It is said by those who attended this treaty that the Indians, in parting with and making sale of the above lands to the whites, did so with much reluctance, and after the treaty was signed, many of them wept."

Their tears would mark the end of the frontier era, and the beginning of Cleveland's West Side, for the Connecticut Land Co. promptly surveyed the west side of the Cuyahoga, calling the area Brooklyn Township.

This is how an early historian described that area: "On the west side of the river, opposite St. Clair St., where the Indians had a ferry, a trail led out across the marshy ground, up the hill past the old log trading house, where there were springs of water, to an opening in the forest, near the crossing of Pearl and Detroit Sts. In this pleasant space the savages practiced their games, held their pow-wows, and when whiskey could be procured, enjoyed themselves while it lasted."

This idyllic scene would begin to end in the spring of 1812, when a certain James Fish and family made a 47-day journey from Connecticut in an ox-drawn wagon to the new Brooklyn territory, where they built a log house for $18 and set up housekeeping. Next year, Ozias Brainard and family arrived. They must have liked it because the following spring, more Brainards, a Hinckley, and a Young family—six families in all—came to stay.

To the jealous Clevelanders this was "an avalanche of emigrants." Township trustees decided that these new families were so dirt-poor that Cleveland Township would probably have to be taxed to support them, and were about to send a constable across the river to evict the new West Siders, "to drive the invaders out of town."

Alonzo Carter, son of Cleveland's most famous citizen, Lorenzo Carter, heard of the move and put a stop to it. In fact, Alonzo said, the alleged paupers were worth more than all the trustees of Cleveland, combined! The Carter name was still magic in Cleveland, and that was the end of the opposition.

In 1825, Alonzo Carter ended up being a West Side resident when a new, direct channel for the river was cut right across his farm, separating eight acres from the East Side. Alonzo's cabin was on that opposite shore facing the foot of Superior Ave.

But the damage was done; West Siders wouldn't forget this incident and the feud would go on long after people forgot the reason for its beginning.

Life Could Be Rough During Pioneer Days

New England farmers around the turn of the 19th century had an idealized version of life in the newly opened Western Reserve lands in Ohio. They had visions of cheap and fertile lands instead of the hardscrabble, thin soil they broke their backs over in Connecticut and Vermont. They could picture woods full of game to supplement a hearty diet from their crops.

The Connecticut Land Co., which owned much of what is now northeastern Ohio, didn't exactly disabuse them of their notions. After all, it wanted to unload at a profit the 3 million acres it bought from the state of Connecticut.

The reality, though, was vastly different.

When settlers arrived in the reserve after a killing journey over roads hacked out of the forest, the bitter reality set in quickly.

After building some sort of shelter, the men would spend their entire days in the field getting in a crop.

And the women? They washed clothes for huge families, made raw cloth from cotton and flax, cooked, churned butter—work that turned young girls into old, worn-out women in a few years.

The log cabins were so crude that one settler said, "We hung up a quilt, and that, with a big bulldog, constituted the door."

Here's what Mrs. Joel Thorp did when she found herself alone with three small children in their Cleveland log cabin after her husband left to look for food for his starving family.

First, she looked, unsuccessfully, in the cracks of the logs for a few kernals of corn; then, she emptied her straw mattress on the ground and picked it over to get a few mouthfuls of wheat that she boiled and gave to the kids.

Finally, with her heart hammering in terror that she would miss, she used their last musket ball to shoot a wild turkey, which kept them alive until her husband got home!

Even 20 years later, a visiting doctor, Zerah Hawley, reported visiting sick children in one-room log cabins that didn't even have a fireplace or a chimney—the fire was built right against the cabin logs and the smoke escaped through a hole in the roof.

A more prosperous two-room cabin meant that the hogs and the cows lived in the second room.

Some of the young women, said Hawley, according to historian Harlan Hatcher, "dock the hair square behind, leaving it about six inches long, which gives them a very uncouth and forbidding appearance."

Hawley had dinner with one pioneer family: They had one knife and one fork which they gave to him.

The others ate with a shoe knife and an old razor blade with a wooden handle. Food was served in a single large dish in the middle of the table.

Under these often grim circumstances, settlers took their fun where they could get it, and tiny little Cleveland saw its chance to become a party town on the Fourth of July, 1801, when all the local citizenry decided to hold a "grand ball."

Since there were only a few cabins down by the Cuyahoga River, the choice of a ballroom was easy: Major Lorenzo Carter's two-room log house on the hill near the corner of Union and Superior lanes.

The elite of that frontier community was there—12 women and 20 men—and they danced to the fiddle of the Master of Ceremonies, Major Samuel Jones.

Gilman Bryant was there; his father had set up Cleveland's first whiskey still and cut the first mill-stones in the area.

He described, many years later, his date with one of Nathaniel Doan's daughters, whom he took to the party: "I waited on Miss Doan, who had just arrived at the Corners, four miles east of town. I was then about 17 years of age, and Miss Doan about fourteen.

"I was dressed in the then style—a gingham suit—my hair queued with one-and-a-half yards of black ribbon, about as long and as thick as a corncob, with a little tuft at the lower end; and for the want of pomatum, I had a little piece of candle rubbed on my hair, and then as much flour as could stay without falling off.

"I had a good wool hat and a pair of brogans that would help to play 'Fisher's Hornpipe,' or 'Hie, Bettie Martin,' when I danced. . . .

"Notwithstanding the floors were of rough puncheons, and their best beverage was made of maple sugar, hot water and whiskey, probably no celebration of American independence was more joyous than this."

The next time you fly to Cleveland and see thousands of lights down below, think of that lonely cabin in the middle of the wilderness and the sound of a fiddle floating over the trackless forests as Gilman Bryant and his friends fought off the terrible loneliness of the frontier with Cleveland's first party.

O'Mic Hanging Reinforced American Indians' Fears

On June 26, 1812, the tiny log-cabin village of Cleveland was experiencing its first traffic jam. The occasion was the public hanging of a convicted murderer, and settlers were pouring in from all over the Western Reserve, and even western Pennsylvania for the event. On the northwest corner of Public Square, where cattle grazed and small boys played on the muddy, stump-filled streets, a gallows had been erected to carry out the execution of a 21-year-old Indian, with the improbable name of John O'Mic.

O'Mic had been in trouble since age 16, when he tangled with the last man in the reserve he should have picked on—Maj. Lorenzo Carter, part-time lawman, hunter, tracker, tavern-keeper, entrepreneur, first citizen of Cleveland. The young brave had threatened Mrs. Carter with a knife when she caught him raiding her vegetable garden. Only O'Mic's father could save his life when the major tracked him down with blood in his eye; O'Mic Sr. promised Carter that his son wouldn't darken Cleveland's muddy streets again.

Five years later, on April 3, 1812, two white trappers were murdered in their sleep and their furs and traps stolen, near Sandusky. John O'Mic was one of the three young Indian braves arrested for the murders. One committed suicide, one was freed because of his extreme youth, and John O'Mic was returned to Cleveland and placed in the custody of Carter to await his trial.

With no jail or courthouse as of yet, Carter took O'Mic to his large cabin and tied him to a rafter in the attic. The trial took place in late April in open-air court under the shade of a large oak tree at the corner of Water and Superior streets, where the verdict was: Guilty of first-degree murder of Daniel Buell who had been killed "with a certain tomahawk, made of iron and steele."

Sentence: Death by hanging.

O'Mic was openly contemptuous of the "palefaces" fear of death

and decided to meet his fate without fear! When word of his at-
titude spread throughout the territory, the settlers poured in to see
for themselves from every forest clearing for many miles around.
Bottles were passed freely—it was a grand, festive occasion for
these entertainment-starved people.

Not everybody felt this way. Mrs. Julia Long, the wife of Cleveland's only doctor, remembered playing with O'Mic when they were
both small children in Painesville. "Why should I wish to see my old
playmate die?" she asked. "I got out of the crowd as quickly as possible and went home."

When the prisoner, the sheriff and Carter ascended the gallows
ladder, the crowd was silent. Suddenly, O'Mic, whose hands were
loosely tied, grabbed a corner post and held on, deperately. Carter,
who spoke his dialect, scolded him for behaving like an old squaw.

O'Mic listened gravely, and promised that if he could have a
half-pint of whiskey, he would go peacefully. The condemned man
downed his cup in one swallow and then grabbed his corner post
again, and held on for what literally was his life, while the drunken
crowd roared. Again, Carter negotiated with the terrified young
man. And again, more whiskey was the answer; and this time, the
last pint was his last pint—the body swung free in the breeze.

A sudden, fierce summer storm blew in off Lake Erie, the crowd
scattered as the sheriff and Carter buried the corpse in a shallow
grave—or did they? The next morning, the body was gone from its
rude coffin. Had O'Mic lived to escape to the western forests?

No, Mrs. Long years later supplied the answer in her diary. Her
husband, Dr. David Long, Dr. Allen, and several other reserve physicians had dug up the body and toted it away at night on their
backs, stumbling, laughing, with lightning flashing, and thunder
booming—and perhaps with more than enough of that same
whiskey inside of them that O'Mic had drunk. Cadavers were in
short supply on the frontier, and Cleveland's once and future great
medical community wanted that body for study.

There were others in the crowd that grim day who never forgot
the spectacle of drunken settlers jeering at a doomed, young
Indian. They were the American Indian tribes that lived west of
the Cuyahoga. And as war clouds were gathering that year between
Great Britain and the United States, the Indians would believe the

British who said that the Americans were always going to be the enemy of the Indian—and they would think of revenge on that small, log-cabin village called Cleveland.

Perry Drives British from Lake Erie

The War of 1812 is one of those half-forgotten wars in American history. The results were inconclusive and left the raw young country with very little to cheer about.

But for the little log-cabin village of Cleveland, it was a life-or-death matter. Villagers weren't concerned about an invasion of British troops. The fear was of a British-inspired Indian attack on this thinly settled, undefended part of the western frontier.

There might have been a collective guilty conscience operating here, also. Just a few weeks before the war broke out, a boisterous crowd had watched the hanging in Public Square of an Indian convicted of murdering white trappers.

Congress declared war on Great Britain June 18, 1812; 10 days later, an express rider galloped into Cleveland with the news from Washington. Cleveland's and Newburgh's militias promptly formed—50 men each—every man in his own "citizen suit," and with his own rifle or shotgun.

By August, the whole linchpin of America's western frontier defense collapsed when Gen. William Hull surrendered Detroit to the British. Cleveland panicked. Rumors of British warships on Lake Erie and British offers inciting Indians to the warpath sent the citizens running for the hills of rival villages.

But 30 Clevelanders swore they would die rather than give up their tiny Fort Huntington, on the bluff where W. 3rd St. and Lakeside Ave. meet. Julianna Long, Dr. David Long's wife, and two other women wouldn't abandon the garrison. She "could nurse the sick and wounded, encourage and comfort those who could fight; at any rate, she would not by her example, encourage disgraceful flight."

By June 1813, it began to look like the garrison might have to live up to its vow when two British warships appeared off the mouth of the Cuyahoga to bombard the shipworks along the shore. Cleveland shipbuilders had been cutting down the dense forests around the village for lake schooners and had supplied the Navy with the

Oliver Hazard Perry took his battle flag and was rowed to "The Niagara," where he continued the Battle of Lake Erie. *(Library of Congress)*

60-ton brig "Ohio," a strong addition to Commodore Perry's Lake Erie fleet.

British firepower was about to put an end to this war industry when Lake Erie came through with one of its notorious summer squalls. Crashing waves pounded the hulls of the British ships, rattled their masts, and probably their morale, too. The next morning, when a thick fog lifted off the lake, the British were gone.

They were next heard from Sept. 10, 1813, when Oliver Hazard Perry's fleet, with heavier guns, took them on in Put-in-Bay off Sandusky in the famous Battle of Lake Erie. Clevelanders swore afterward they could hear the cannon fire 60 miles away. His message to Gen. William Henry Harrison, commander in chief of the northwestern army, reflects his pride and exuberance: "We have met the enemy and they are ours, two ships, two brigs, one schooner and one sloop."

The battle became legend, and the victory lifted the British threat from the Great Lakes.

When peace came in 1814, Cleveland went wild. Public Square was packed with an excited, drunken, noisy crowd.

Another era ended that same year. Lorenzo Carter, Cleveland's real founder, frontiersman, trader and adventurer, would die, and one of those dynamic Connecticut Yankees, Alfred Kelly, would lead Cleveland into a new, exciting future.

It certainly didn't look that way at the time. Kelly had come to the village in 1810, became the first practicing attorney, and was elected to the state legislature in 1814. He quickly saw to it that Cleveland was incorporated as a village, which at the time extended from Erie (E. 9th St.) west to the Cuyahoga, and Huron St. north to the lake.

It still looked like a transplanted New England village with its frame houses set around Public Square, no more or less important than say, Lorain or Sandusky. In fact, the rivers in the latter two towns worked a lot better than the Cuyahoga. A sandbar reached out from the eastern shore of Lake Erie, blocked the harbor and forced ships to unload their cargoes offshore. The water at the river mouth was 3 to 4 feet, motionless, filled with trash and garbage—a breeding ground for typhoid fever, cholera and malaria.

Here's what the future great educator Harvey Rice would say about his arrival in September 1824, on a schooner from Buffalo: "A sand-bar prevented the schooner from entering the river . . . The jolly boat was let down . . . and we were rowed over the sandbar into the placid waters of the river, and landed on the end of a row of planks that stood on stilts and bridged the marshy brink of the river, to the foot of Union Lane. Here we were left standing with our trunks on the wharf-end of a plank at midnight, strangers in a strange land."

Rice describes Public Square as "begemmed with stumps, while near its center glowed its crowning jewel, a log courthouse. The eastern border of the Square was skirted by the native forest, which abounded in rabbits and squirrels, and afforded the villagers a 'happy hunting-ground.' The entire population at that time didn't exceed 400 souls. The town, even at that time, was proud of itself, and called itself, the 'Gem of the West.'"

A year later, in 1825, Congress would vote funds for clearing the river and harbor, which would make a phenomenal difference, but it would be awhile before Cleveland would become a gem of the West.

Early Cleveland Schools
Set Up in Log Cabins

When Ohio became a state in 1803, the state constitution incorporated the marvelous words of the Northwest Ordinance of 1787 regarding education: "Religion, modesty, knowledge, being necessary
to good government and the happiness of mankind, schools and the
means of education shall forever be encouraged."

The federal government, which was land-rich (if cash-poor),
was glad to help with land grants for elementary schools, and Ohio
became the first state given grants for state universities. The Ohio
Legislature provided for setting aside and leasing land in each
township for school purposes, but not the means of local or general
taxation to support education. So, like their modern descendants,
Clevelanders were all for education in theory, but nobody wanted to
pay the necessary taxes.

You might have thought that Moses Cleaveland's Connecticut
Land Co., with one-third of its trustees being Yale grads, mixed in
with a few stray Harvards, would have been interested in promot-
ing culture as several other Ohio land companies had, but the Connecticut was happy enough to unload the land and walk away from
additional expenses.

But rough-and-ready Clevelanders were feeling a twinge of New
England conscience regarding their kids' education, and in 1802,
Anna Spafford gathered about a dozen youngsters in the front room
of Maj. Lorenzo Carter's log cabin and began teaching the 3 R's—
there wasn't any demand in this primitive economy for anything
more sophisticated than that; however, Spafford did have an ex-
tracurricular course: She would teach her students "how to shoot."

Nathaniel Doan's daughter, Sara, did the same thing on "the
Ridge Road" (which later became Euclid Ave.). Her school was
probably near Doan's Corners (now E. 105th St. and Euclid).

Here's a description of an early Cleveland schoolhouse: "A log
cabin with a rough stone chimney; a foot or two cut here and there
to admit the light, with greased paper over the openings; a large

The first schoolhouse in Cleveland. *(CSU)*

fireplace; a puncheon floor; a few benches made of split logs with the flat side up, and a well-developed birch rod over the master's seat. A teacher, who as late as 1813 received $10 per month, was looked upon as receiving good wages."

He also had to "agree to keep six hours in each day, and to keep good order in said school." "Good order" was kept with a wooden paddle, which had an alphabet on one side and the multiplication table on the other, when it wasn't being used as an enforcer.

In 1816, 27 citizens felt they could afford something better than log-cabin schoolhouses, and they ponied up from $2.50 to $20 each for a total of almost $200 to build a frame schoolhouse on St. Clair Ave. near Bank St. (now W. 6th St.). The windows were deliberately placed high so the children couldn't be distracted from their studies by looking outside. An early sketch shows several boys and girls playing in the schoolyard—one boy is walking on stilts.

The Cleveland village trustees bought out the founders a year later, refunding their money, but admission wasn't free, "except to a few who were too poor to pay tuition." Single men were compelled to pay tuition for these poor children, apparently on the presumption that they were rolling in money since they didn't have to support families.

Cleveland Academy opened across the street on St. Clair in 1822—a two-story brick building—under the direction of the Rev. William McLean. Tuition for a 12-week term broke down to $1.75 for reading, spelling and writing; grammar and geography were another dollar, with Greek, Latin and higher mathematics packaged at $4.

It remained for a Williams College graduate named Harvey Rice to play godfather to Cleveland's and Ohio's public schools. He arrived at the mouth of the Cuyahoga on a schooner from Buffalo in September 1825, along with a companion.

The next day he was appointed principal and teacher of classics at the Academy.

Although Rice gave up teaching for the law a year later, he never gave up his involvement with education. In 1851 he was elected to the state Senate, where he introduced the bill that created the common school system of Ohio: "By the provisions of this bill, it is intended to make our common schools what they ought to be— the colleges of the people—'cheap enough for the poorest, and good enough for the richest.'

By the Civil War, public schools had almost entirely replaced the private academies of those earlier days.

Ushering In the Erie Canal

How The Waterway Changed Cleveland

There's a famous scene in the movie "The Graduate" in which young college graduate Dustin Hoffman is advised by his parents' friend to get into plastics.

Well, back in the 1820s, in struggling little Cleveland, Ohio, young men were perhaps being advised to get into that era's cutting edge of technology—canals! It was safe, cheap and seemed to promise the opening up of the whole interior of the raw young state.

True, there were bumpy roads that had been hacked through the forest connecting Cleveland with Columbus and Pittsburgh by stagecoach, but they only carried passengers. They were expensive and uncomfortable to boot.

The gleam in the Ohio legislature's eye was the great new Erie Canal, completed in 1825. It was the first in the country, connecting Lake Erie with the Hudson River and New York City. Hundreds of thousands of immigrants were already pouring into the virgin Northwest, not only from soil-poor New England, but directly from Europe. Ending their Erie Canal journey at Buffalo, they were shipping out from there to Ohio, Michigan and Indiana, looking for fertile land.

The Ohio legislature was considering a north-south 309-mile canal route from Lake Erie down to Portsmouth that would revolutionize commerce and travel in the state; and whichever lake port got the northern terminus was going to boom beyond any civic booster's wildest dreams!

But why Cleveland for this wonderful award? In 1820 there were still only 606 hardy souls who called themselves Clevelanders (unless you counted the real natives, some of whom were still living along the Cuyahoga). Cows were still meandering among the tree stumps on Public Square. The harbor was miserably clogged with sandbars, and lake schooners had to unload their cargoes on lighters and then reload them farther down the Cuyahoga where the

Boats on the Lake Erie and Ohio River Canals were powered by horses and mules in the late 19th century. *(CSU)*

river was deep enough to handle them; not to mention the malaria, cholera and typhoid that plagued the harbor area.

Now, take Sandusky—there was a town with a real, honest-to-goodness harbor. And what about Ashtabula, with its fine river? Or Painesville, or Lorain—all bigger and much more prosperous than the Forest City—which was still one of the state's smallest towns some 25 years after its founding.

Cleveland had a man to match the challenge—Alfred Kelley. And Kelley wanted—and would get—Cleveland for the northern canal terminus.

Kelley had come to Cleveland village in 1810, brought his father and brothers a year later, and then proceeded to organize everything within sight of his new home. He became the town's first practicing attorney, and prosecuting attorney on his 21st birthday.

In 1814, the year the great pioneer Lorenzo Carter died, Kelley was elected to the state legislature where he was responsible for Cleveland's prompt incorporation as a village. Quite naturally, he was elected president by all 12 trustees. When he resigned a year later, the village must have liked the Kelley touch because they appointed his father the next president.

Alfred Kelley became so influential in the state legislature that he was appointed to the Ohio Canal Commission when they first surveyed the canal project in 1822, and quickly came to dominate it. There was never any question of any alternate route for Kelley—he wanted Cleveland, and that was that.

He gave up his law practice to work for $3 per day, tirelessly tramping through malarial swamps and woods, politicking with small-town mayors who wanted their towns to be canal ports, working with warehousemen and shippers, fighting with contractors to keep them to the letter of their commitments. Some contractors refused to work for him—too tough, they said, not willing to bend a little. In the end, he wrecked his health and shortened his life.

Work on the first section of the canal from Cleveland to Akron started in 1825, and it would revolutionize Cleveland with its first ethnic mix. Several thousand Irish and German workmen poured into the sleepy little village of New England farmers. Many of them had been skilled workmen from the Erie Canal—grubbers, muckers, ditchers, mechanics, engineers and executives. They had to be housed and fed, and the village began to stir.

The newcomers first cleared the ground in the Cuyahoga Valley, then dug the great ditch, 26 feet wide at the bottom, sloping outward to a 40-foot width. Others mined and shaped the stone for the locks that would raise and lower the boats. For 30 cents a day they blasted through solid rock, cut down forests, fell sick and died from the heat and disease.

Finally, in July of 1827, the 37-mile stretch between Cleveland and Akron was opened with a tremendous celebration featuring boats parading on the Cuyahoga, cannon firing, banquets, speeches and a grand ball. Alfred Kelley proposed the 16th—count 'em—16th toast that evening in Belden's Tavern to: "The people of the state of Ohio."

And Cleveland was now going to become the leading commercial town in that state—the great receiving port for barges filled with wheat, butter, tobacco, lumber and leather from the interior; in return, the city would ship down fish, grindstones, cloth, pig iron and tools.

Leave plastics to the future! Young people—come to Cleveland now!

How a City is Forged

It Was Ships, Coal and Iron

On New Year's Day 1822, the Cleveland Herald ran an editorial on a remarkably modern subject: "Our country has run ahead of her income; acknowledges her financial deficiencies, and has committed her credit to the ordeal of such as have been willing to put it to the test, but she holds high expectations of her future destinies; means to continue steadfast at the watchtower in view of better times, and intends to live to see a return of the golden days of prosperity."

You could have learned from the same newspaper that while Pennsylvania banks were 100 percent sound, there wasn't a single Ohio bank whose notes were quoted at par; they were discounted anywhere from 1 percent to 75 percent.

As a matter of fact, the Herald itself complained that it had troubles with slow collections.

The problem dated back to the War of 1812, which the federal government financed with worthless paper money, throwing the nation's financial system into chaos.

Hard money was so scarce in Cleveland that the village trustees issued corporation scrip, popularly known as "shinplasters," ranging in value from 6.25 cents to 50 cents.

The rare silver dollar was divided into eight pieces, each passing for a shilling—in other words, 12.5 cents. Barter was a common way to deal; there wasn't a merchant who wouldn't take pork, whiskey, flour or beeswax in exchange for his goods.

Finally Congress stabilized the country by establishing the Second Bank of the United States; Cleveland was slated to have a branch in their new Commercial Bank of Lake Erie, just chartered by the state in 1816, and the village's pioneer bank.

The bank's officers were all the local heavy-hitters, names like Alfred Kelley, president, with Miles, Doan, Taylor, Long, Williamson and Strong as trustees.

Prominent businessman and attorney Leonard
Case, Sr., planted many of the trees that would
earn Cleveland the nickname "The Forest City."
(Cleveland Public Library)

A certain Leonard Case was brought in from Warren because he "wrote a good hand and was a good accountant," at a salary of $800 a year.

Case was the son of a poor, frontier farmer who had moved his family to Warren in 1800. Leonard Case was left crippled and in pain for the rest of his life the following year when he suffered from extreme exposure.

But there was no keeping Case down. He worked as a clerk for Cleveland's founding company, the Connecticut Land Co., and studied law. During the War of 1812, he collected delinquent taxes for areas of the Western Reserve.

As the bank's cashier, he still found time to practice law and deal in real estate; not unusual for the times, since most prominent Clevelanders were involved in each other's ventures—shipping, warehousing, building, tavern-keeping.

The Commercial Bank failed in 1820; when it re-organized and resumed business in 1832, it paid off all its liabilities to the treasurer of the United States, less than $10,000.

Somehow, infant industry was stirring under the surface in the bucolic little village by the lake as early as 1820, "shinplaster" financing or not.

Lake schooners had been built on the Cuyahoga River for at

least 10 years by then. Noble Merwin launched a 44-ton schooner at the foot of Superior St. in March 1822, with this difference: Her chain cable was one of Cleveland's first homemade products. The blacksmith tested its quality and strength by wrapping it around a tree and pulling on it with teams of oxen.

"When she was launched," said Merwin's son George, "I stood on the heel of her bowsprit, and as she touched the water, christened her by giving her my mother's name, 'Minerva,' and broke a jug of whiskey over her bows . . . "

The first Cleveland steamship was built by Levi Johnson in 1824, but its 60-70 horsepower motor had to be built in Pittsburgh. There were no iron foundries in town.

Blacksmiths like Nathaniel Doan could repair a kettle or a tool, but that was the limit of local technology.

By 1827, at Detroit and Center streets in the Flats, a small foundry called the Cuyahoga Steam Furnace Co. started up. Seven years later, it became the first local incorporated business, growing into an outfit that produced 500 tons of castings a year, and employing 100 workers.

By the 1840s, the company was making screw propellers for lake schooners, plows, axes, the first railroad locomotive west of the Alleghenies, and cannons for the U.S. Army.

One of the reasons that the iron and steel business got started in Cleveland was the availability of coal, and what was mistakenly thought of as an "abundance" of iron ore in the Western Reserve.

Henry Newberry, in 1828, had dug some coal from his farm in Cuyahoga Falls and tried to peddle it to Cleveland housewives; he wasn't very successful because of the clean-burning wood right out in their back yards.

But Newberry was finally given a chance to try his heating product in the lobby of the Franklin House Hotel, where it made a hit with the guests; word spread to local blacksmiths, and from there to the small industries in the Flats.

By the time William Otis set up his foundry in 1840, the demand for iron had begun to outstrip the local supply of ore. It took only $557 worth of capital to give one of his workmen the tools, machines and facilities to work a 70-hour week.

The giant that would become famous worldwide as "Cleveland Industry," was on its way.

Practicing Medicine in the Western Reserve

U.S. Senator Stanley Griswold, newly appointed from Ohio, was on his way to Washington in 1809. He took the time to write a friend who was inquiring about whether the Cleveland area could support a physician: "I have consulted with the principal characters, particularly Judge Walworth, who concurs with me, that Cleveland would be an excellent place for a young physician, and cannot long remain unoccupied. This is based more on what the place is expected to be, than what it is . . . settlements are scattered, and roads new and bad, which would make it a painful practice . . . " (The letter was wrong about the roads being "new and bad"—they were nonexistent.)

How good a practice could you have with only a few hundred people spread out in a 50-mile area, most of whom had to pay in produce? The letter went on to warn any prospects, "A young physician will be certain to succeed, but for a short time, if without means, must keep school . . . till a piece of ground, bring in a few goods, or do something else in connection with his practice." In short, medicine in the Western Reserve was a part-time profession, and a young doctor had better think about moonlighting.

A year later, Dr. David Long, 23, arrived like Lancelot when he heard that call. (As a matter of fact, he soon married Judge Walworth's daughter, Julianna.) He had studied with his uncle, a country doctor, and had the additional—and very rare—certificate from four months spent at the College of Physicians & Surgery in New York City. It evidently didn't take any longer than that to cover the entire range of medical knowledge of the day, which consisted of how to bleed a patient, blister, or prescribe emetics, calomel, or antimony.

Whether Long needed the money or was simply an entrepreneurial type, he immediately became a founder of the first company to build a pier to handle lake shipping which had to be manhandled over sandbars at the mouth of the Cuyahoga River in 1816; quicksands and storms soon put an end to that move. He was one of the

David Long, Cleveland's first black physician.
(Cleveland Public Library)

trustees of the pioneer Commercial Bank of Lake Erie that same year—the one that lasted two years; and a partner in a warehouse.

He didn't neglect the community, either as benefactor or politician, being a founder of the Episcopal church in 1820, a county commissioner, and village mayor in 1829.

But no matter how competent or community-minded a physician of that day might be, he couldn't protect Cleveland village from the killer diseases that lurked around every corner in early 19th century America: cholera, malaria, and typhoid.

The Cleveland-to-Akron 37-mile stretch of the Ohio Canal had no sooner been dedicated in 1827, when typhoid fever struck the mostly Irish workers who had been digging the basin in malarial swamps, killing 17 men in July and August. "A terrible depression of spirits and stagnation of business ensued," said early settler Ara Sprague. "People were generally discouraged and anxious to leave." In May 1832, panic spread through the Great Lakes region when cholera from Canada struck. Cleveland village appointed a board of health, headed by Dr. David Long, to inspect ships and isolate sick people who might come into the harbor.

That summer, an American troop ship, the Henry Clay, on its way to Chicago to fight Indians, had to stop near Detroit and disembark all the well soldiers because of an outbreak. When ship's captain Norton tried to obtain food and medicine at Detroit to take his sick soldiers back to Buffalo, he was driven off by heavily armed townsmen. Six more men had died and the rest were too ill to work the steamer when the Henry Clay appeared on June 10th on the west bank of the Cuyahoga, flying a flag of distress.

Some Clevelanders panicked—they wanted to go down and burn her. Capt. Norton had to disguise himself to go ashore while the ship was fumigated. But the mayor and David Long's board of health got the sick soldiers off and into barracks on Whiskey Island, supplying food and courageous doctors. When the hospital ran short of fresh water, another ship's captain filled two casks at a spring near Superior St. and rowed them down the river to the barracks.

But cholera struck the village anyway, including those who had worked at Whiskey Island and those who hadn't gone near it. Fifty more citizens died that month before the disease was spent.

Life in early Cleveland could be fresh and clean as the unpolluted air filling the sails of schooners on Lake Erie . . . and it also could be deadly.

When Cleveland Almost Went
a Bridge Too Far

Like two Balkan nations, Cleveland and Ohio City existed in a state of uneasy truce in 1837; but there was big trouble brewing, and it was coming to a head over a bridge.

In 1822, when the Cuyahoga River could only be crossed by boat, the towns jointly built a float bridge from the foot of Detroit Ave. to the foot of Superior St. That was the end of their cooperation, however.

A few years later, the Ohio Canal opened and created a boom for both communities. The river banks were lined with forwarding and commission houses, ship chandlers, merchants and artisans. Hundreds of wagons of produce from the south and west would run along Pearl Rd. and pass through Ohio City before crossing over the jointly owned float bridge at the foot of Detroit to ship their goods out of the port of Cleveland.

West Side merchants and saloons prospered as much as their East Side counterparts when more than 1,900 sailing vessels and steamboats would weigh in at Cleveland Harbor in a year's time.

Cleveland grew to a population of 6,000 by 1836, with little Ohio City at 2,000, but when both communities raced to become the first city incorporated in Cuyahoga County, the West Side won the title by a few days. All the old bitterness emerged.

There were other needles under East Siders' skins: West Side developers were planning an 80-acre development in the Flats and were talking of digging another channel from the river so they could have their own harbor. They built a fine five-story hotel, the Ohio City Exchange, which came to dominate the whole area socially. The hotel's dome lights were kept lighted all night, serving as a landmark and a guide for ships coming into Cleveland Harbor.

Some East Siders, with an appalling lack of civic loyalty, were scheduling banquets and balls in the great new edifice. New arrivals in the Western Reserve were bypassing the East Side and buying desirable West Side lots just like in the old pioneer days.

Cleveland's first mayor, John Willey.
(Cleveland Public Library)

Then two buccaneering real estate speculators brought things to an explosive head. James Clark and his partner, Cleveland's first city mayor, John Willey, bought up land ringing Ohio City to the south and west, built improvements on it, and extended Columbus St. from the West Side to the Cuyahoga River south of the Detroit Ave. float bridge.

There, for $15,000, they built a roofed, enclosed drawbridge. The city director proclaimed, "This splendid bridge was presented to the corporation of Cleveland by the owners with the express stipulation that it should remain forever free for the accommodation of the public . . ."

Traffic from the south could now be led up to Ontario and Prospect streets, where the partners had built commercial properties called Cleveland Centre. This may have had something to do with their high-minded community spirit.

To encourage the traffic bypass even more, Cleveland City Council (remember, Willey was the mayor) directed the removal of the Cleveland half of the Detroit Ave. float bridge.

"This act was performed one night while the Ohio citizens lay dreaming of future municipal greatness," historian James Kennedy wrote 100 years ago. "And when the morning mists arose from over the valley of the Cuyahoga, they saw their direct communication gone, and realized that to reach the courthouse and other points of interest in Cleveland, they would be compelled to travel southward, and make use of the hated Columbus St. bridge."

At dawn the first morning the bridge section was gone, horse-drawn wagons from the West Side had to be desperately reined in before they plunged into the river.

Now the dogs of war were let loose. "Two bridges or none!" became the West Side war cry. The Ohio City marshal and his deputies tried to dynamite their end of the Columbus St. bridge; when that fizzled, 1,000 West Siders descended on it with picks, axes, clubs and muskets, and were busily ripping up planks when the Cleveland militia arrived to join the melee.

Shots were fired, heavy blows exchanged. Fortunately, the Cuyahoga County sheriff called a halt to the battle before anyone was killed.

The courts eventually settled the matter in favor of two bridges, and both towns have mixed freely ever since.

Herald of the News

The First Papers Were Lively

Frontier newspapers were lively, lusty and brawling, and Cleveland's first was no exception.

In July 1818, The Cleaveland Gazette & Commercial Register appeared as a weekly aimed at all 172 of Cleveland's official residents and the county population, too. The newspaper office, on the north side of Superior just west of Public Square, housed the entire staff of editor, publisher, printers, and newsboys—all rolled up into one person, Andrew Logan.

He had arrived from Beaver, Pa., with a hand press and type that was so worn-out the printing was almost illegible. A subscription was $2 a year, if paid in advance, or $3, if you had some qualms about the paper's future. Logan himself was a small, dark man who was believed to be a descendant of the famous Mingo Indian chief, Logan.

Headlines screamed "Shocking Murder," and "The Sea Serpent Again!" but it was the editorial commentary, in the 19th century always inextricably mixed with the news itself, that would make or break the newspapers of the day.

Logan viciously attacked the just-chartered U.S. Bank, but strongly backed the building of the Erie Canal across New York State, and the invasion of Florida by U.S. troops. And there were reports of struggles against dictators in Mexico and South America, and in case you had any doubts as to where editor Logan stood on such issues, a featured quotation was Tom Paine's "Where liberty dwells, there is my country."

Cleveland itself had some important news, including the first recorded ordinance. It provided that "if any person shall shoot or discharge any gun or pistol within said village, such person so offending, shall upon conviction, be fined in any sum not exceeding five dollars, nor under 50 cents, for the use of the said village."

Also, in 1818; 21 boats entered or cleared the harbor for Buffalo

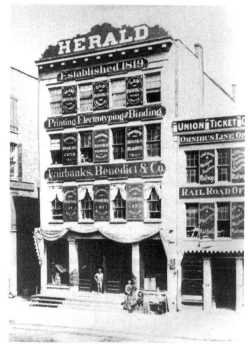

The offices of the Herald, 1873. *(CSU)*

or Detroit during one week in July and the schooner "American Eagle" arrived with "six families of Irish, 47 passengers, 3 months from Ireland." The ethnic mix was just beginning.

But after publishing on-and-off for about a year, the "Register" disappeared. Although it couldn't have been any consolation to editor Logan, he can be credited with founding Cleveland's great newspaper tradition.

Perhaps a paper shortage sank the Register. Paper arrived unpredictably by wagon from Pittsburgh. Or it may have been competition from a new journal founded in 1819.

Clevelander Eber Howe convinced a friend to move his newspaper from Erie, Pa., to Cleveland, lock, stock and printing-press. The two set up shop on Superior St., next to the Commercial Coffee House, where the big Conestoga wagons stopped on their trips from the East. Howe and friend didn't have a single subscriber, but they must have known their customers' tastes because they built up circulation to 300 people within a few months. The paper was called the Cleaveland Herald.

Howe describes his arduous sales effort: "Each and every week, after the paper had been struck off, I mounted a horse with a valise, filled with copies of the Herald, and distributed them at the doors of all subscribers between Cleveland and Painesville, a distance of 30 miles, leaving a package at the latter place; and on returning diverged two miles to what is known as Kirtland Flats, where another package was left for distribution."

The trip took two days. "I frequently carried a tin horn to notify the yeomanry of the arrival of the latest news," he noted. "This service was performed through the fall, winter, and spring, and through rain, snow, and mud, with only one additional charge of 50 cents on the subscription price . . ."

No wonder Howe quit the paper after two years, moving to Painesville where he opened his own newspaper. His partner at the Herald, a gentleman named Willes, not only continued publication, but had years without a rival. The Herald wrote its own epitaph on March 15, 1885: "We know that in passing out of sight, it will leave behind it a good name, and thousands will mourn its departure, as that of an old, a trusted, a valued friend."

There's nothing you can add to that.

Wild West on Erie

Law, Order Not Early Strong Suit

Judge Earl R. Hoover, writing of the early Western Reserve days, noted that, "An engraved invitation to settle in the Western Reserve was almost an invitation to settle in one's own grave. It was an invitation to fight one's way through a wilderness to arrive at a wilderness surrounded by a wilderness."

Why then would a prosperous New England family leave home to settle in that early wilderness? The answer is simple—not many did. The pioneers who came here usually had literally nothing to lose since they didn't own anything to begin with. This made for a rough-and-ready mix of frontier types that our century usually associates with the Wild West of the 1870s.

Listen to historian Charles Kennedy, writing almost 100 years ago: "It has become a popular impression that the pioneers of not only the Western Reserve, but of all sections where New England elements predominated, were pious and God-fearing men, who had little need of courts or the officers of the law. It is a fact that the strong arm of the law was needed in early northeastern Ohio as elsewhere."

And another early writer: "The first settlers were not generally godly men, such as founded Plymouth, Mass., and Connecticut or even Marietta and Granville, Ohio . . . The first emigration was largely made up of men who desired to throw off the heavy trammels of an old and strongly conservative community, where church and state were closely connected, and where society was dominated by political and religious castes. Still further, the East was at this time swept by an epidemic of land speculation, while the lax moral influence of a removal from an old and well-ordered society to the woods produced its usual effects."

It's recorded that in the Cleveland of 1829, volunteers banded together to preserve law and order and track down horse thieves. Did these "volunteers" become what was known in the West years

This early Cleveland patrol station is evidence that the city's police force had rather humble beginnings. *(CSU)*

later as vigilantes, with the lynch law implied by that word? The old journals don't say; but it is plain that law and order didn't come easily to Cleveland.

It was January of 1836 before a growing crime wave forced the City Council to establish a City Watch that consisted of eight volunteer companies of six men each; they policed the city from sundown to sunrise, each company serving once a month.

The saloons were particularly under surveillance. Cleveland seems to have been awash in cheap, Monongahela rye whiskey with plenty of thirsty, rowdy, customers. Every wharf in the Flats had its "groceries," selling liquor to the tough bargemen and passengers from the Ohio Canal boats.

According to the "Whig" newspaper in October of that year, the race course established in 1835 encouraged "a flood of imported depravity, strengthened by all the canaille that could be mustered from groceries and other dens of pollution."

By 1853, things were getting out of hand again; there were only four acting officers and a half-dozen watchmen to protect a town of 17,000 plus. The Plain Dealer commented on the free-and-easy flow of hard liquor: "Our government lands cost $1 an acre on an average, and champagne $42 a bottle. How many a man dies in the poorhouse, who, during his lifetime, has drank a fertile township, trees and all."

An idea of the kinds of crimes being committed comes from the docket of Cleveland's first Police Court set up in April 1853. The court was in a small backroom in the so-called Gaylord Block, on Superior between Seneca Ave., now W. 3rd St., and Public Square, and the judge didn't have a bench—just a small desk. The first sentence handed down was for a $5 fine against each of five playful firemen who were fined for "getting up a false alarm of fire."

Then, in other cases heard, there was "immoderate driving in the street," "selling unwholesome meat," "forestalling market," "soliciting guests drunk," and, "a breach of the peace by disturbing a ball at Kelly's hall" (which sounds like gate-crashing). Not the kind of police docket you would see in any city in America today; just that old devil whiskey, mixed with greed behind most of the crimes.

But the Civil War and Industrial Revolution would change the face of all American cities forever. Crime would become more like what we are too familiar with today. In 1866 Cleveland citizens were so disturbed by increasingly violent crimes that City Council established a metropolitan police force with a board of police commissioners.

An old print from that summer of '66 shows two patrolmen walking their beat on Public Square, wearing badges, striped trousers, straw hats, nightsticks in hand. The trees are in full bloom, and a few carriages are trotting along Superior. The violent labor strikes of the '80s and the 1930s, Elliot Ness, Danny Green, Hough riots, Glenville—all were still far in the future of the forces of law and order on that sunny, summer day.

Fire Engine Ruckus

Trustees Lost Jobs in Deal

Early Cleveland homes were built almost exclusively of wood, so fires were an ever-present danger. Volunteers would fight fires by a bucket brigade that drew its water from an 8-foot-wide public well equipped with a wheel and two buckets. It was on Bank St., now W. 6th St., near Superior Ave.

When the village trustees spent either $285 or $400 (the amount isn't certain) on their first fire engine, purchased from the American Hydraulic Co. in 1829, you would have thought the locals would have been grateful. But far from it!

They promptly voted the trustees out of office and formed a volunteer fire company. In 1833, 45 volunteers formed the Live Oak firefighting company, and the village bought a secondhand pumper engine for $700.

But the memory of that earlier chastisement from the voters stuck with trustee John W. Allen. Many years later, here's what he had to say about those spendthrift days: "We thought it expedient to buy a fire engine, and we negotiated for the purpose of purchasing a small engine. We were about to make a contract for the engine, and were to pay $400—$50 down and $350 in a note of the village corporation.

"There was a set of men who were hostile to the measure. They got up at a meeting and talked pretty strongly, intimating that we had joined hands with the engine company to swindle the people here, and that we undoubtedly participated in the plunder.

"But we bought the engine and paid the $50 like honest men, and gave the note of the corporation for the balance. An election intervened the next spring, and we were all turned out, and a new set of men put in who repudiated the note. The note came here for collection, judgment was rendered, and those men had to walk up to the captain's office and settle the bill."

Allen would go on to become mayor, state senator, bank and

Trustee John W. Allen purchased one of the first
fire engines used by the Live Oak firefighting
company. *(Cleveland Public Library)*

railroad president and two-term congressman, but one wonders if
any of his many honors gave him as much satisfaction as that day in
1829 when his political opponents had to foot the bill for the city's
first fire engine.

Two-thirds of the active, unpaid fire department volunteered
in 1861 for service in the Union Army; Cleveland instituted a professional, salaried firefighting force in 1864, equipping it with the
latest steam engines to fight particularly the oil refinery fires that
were smothering the Flats in black, oily smoke.

But the memory of the spirit of the old, volunteer fire companies stayed with one man, at least: George Marshall, who wrote a
history of Cleveland's early fire department about 100 years ago.

Marshall wrote, "It was simply a concentrated manpower, with
willing hands and without horses or steam. It comprised a goodly
share of the young blood of the city—young men with more muscle

than money, men strong of arm and fleet of foot, men who had no other purpose in 'running with the machine' than a desire to do something worthy of their manhood.

"Many young men who had not a farthing in combustible matter at stake, except what covered their backs, or what was at the washer-woman's, were the most active men in the department. They could work with the same vigor to save the poor man's cottage from the flames as the rich man's palace; while on parade days they would march with a more stately tread, and run with greater speed, if they but knew their sweetheart was among the spectators.

"This young city was miserably poor in those days, while there were scattered here and there a pretty good lot of combustible dwellings which needed the supervising care of a well-drilled fire department. The machines were heavy to handle, while the streets, during one-third of the year, were nearly impassable, and the common council forbade the running of fire engines on the sidewalks.

"The entire compensation to volunteers was one dollar each. The real service was performed for the honor and glory of the enterprise, as well as the fun to be had between times of hard work.

"The facilities for obtaining water were not good, and limited to cisterns, the Ohio Canal, and the river. The cisterns were often out of water and out of repair, while some of the engines in trying for water from them were compelled to act like some of our modern political newspapers—they would throw nothing but mud."

One senses that Marshall had had his run-ins with the media.

Rails' Uphill Road

Lone Worker Paved Way

Clevelanders were a pretty smug lot in the early 1830s. The Ohio Canal had turned the once-picturesque little village into a bustling, hustling mercantile town. It linked the produce of the Midwest with the Eastern seaboard through Buffalo and the Erie Canal, bringing manufactured goods and thousands of immigrants back the same way.

There was a hi-tech threat to the canal on the horizon, called "railroads." Cleveland's rival neighbors, Painesville and Sandusky, still smarting from not being chosen as the canal's northern terminus, were determined to get state charters and get their railroads running before Cleveland woke up to the threat.

Painesville, in a petition to the Ohio legislature, said its harbor was as "susceptible of as great, if not greater, improvement as that at Cleveland." The state rejected Painesville's bid—it had enough problems trying to pay off the Ohio Canal debt.

But in a short time, Ohio got caught up in the speculative fever of the times. As a Cleveland historian said, "State legislatures were disposed to grant anything to corporations that promised to create great wealth out of nothing, and when the country was in the wildest state of speculation of that great speculative decade."

So the state got busy chartering railroads, turnpikes, and canals, and anybody could play. A railroad charter even gave a company banking privileges and the right to issue its own paper money.

In 1837, the Ohio legislature made itself a partner in all the crazy, reckless schemes, issuing state-guaranteed bonds to the railroads in the amount of one-third of the capitalization of "companies organized to build railroads," if the companies raised the other two-thirds themselves; the state took the company's stock in return.

Many new companies immediately formed with phony assets and made off with the state's money to the tune of more than $3 million—before this so-called plunder law was repealed in 1840.

But the railroads were going to be built, one way or another, and some prominent Clevelanders got a charter in 1836, good for 10 years, for a Cleveland-Columbus-Cincinnati road—and then, couldn't get the financing.

Even the involvement of men like Leonard Case, Sr., and Thomas Kelley, Alfred's brother,—plus city credit to the tune of $200,000—wasn't enough to overcome the fears of Eastern and foreign banks of being burned. Finally, Alfred Kelley, the great promoter of the Ohio Canal, moved back to Cleveland from Columbus in 1846 to assume the presidency of the company, and his reputation brought in some $3,000,000 from the public.

By the fall of 1847, Kelley had been able to get the 10 year charter limit extended for only one year. It was put-up or shut-up time for Kelley and his prominent friends.

And so it was that one fine October day that year, a dozen men, wearing their best top hats and frock coats, marched down Superior Ave. to River St., together with their one and only employee, and one shovel, one pick, and one wheelbarrow.

Alfred Kelley dug the first chunk of soil, put it in the wheelbarrow, dumped it some yards away, and then solemnly turned his tools over to the other officials, who each took his turn at the digging. "Then," said George Marshall, who was there, "we all shouted a great shout that the road was really inaugurated."

The shovel was then turned over to the one, lone workman, who started digging, and kept at it day after day all that fall and winter of 1847, through rain, sleet, and snow, following a line of stakes. "Foot by foot," said Marshall, "each day the brown earth could be seen gaining on the white snow on the line towards Columbus, and hope remained lively in the breast of everyone that saw the progress, that if the physical powers of that solitary laborer held out long enough, he would some day be able to go to State's prison by rail."

That winter, the driver of the Warren-Pittsburg stagecoach would stop at Pittsburgh St., near the bluff, and explain to his astonished passengers that this one man was single-handedly building a railroad.

As for Alfred Kelley and friends, they scraped, borrowed and donated money. By Feb. 21, 1851, a little wood-burning locomotive, built in the Flats by the Cuyahoga Steam Furnace Co., pulled the first train into Cleveland, from Columbus. Alfred Kelley had done it again.

And that solitary workman? On the next snowy day you're driving down I-71 from Cleveland to Columbus, look hard for him out there in the mists along the road—with his shovel, his pick, and his wheelbarrow.

Monied Class Sparked Growth in the Arts

The opening of the Ohio Canal in 1827 created Cleveland's first successful entrepreneurs in shipping, trading and manufacturing. This new monied class began to look around after a while for some leisure activities and for the prestige that comes with being a patron of the arts.

Not that there had been a vacuum of interest in theater, music and literature. In May 1820, a visiting troupe of professional entertainers performed for a week to sold-out crowds at Mowrey's Tavern in what was billed as the first theatrical performance in Cleveland. People came from all over the Western Reserve and paid their 50 cents to see "The Purse Won the Benevolent Tar" and "The Mountaineers."

A book store and a book bindery opened that same year, and the first work was published by a Cleveland author, a woman who called herself "Catherine Brown, the Converted Cherokee."

Live forums and debates were the entertainment of the era. Topics included "Ought Females of Full Age to Have an Equal Share with Males in the Government of the Nation?" and "Is Love a Stronger Passion than Hatred?"

And then, Cleveland joined the American cultural mainstream in a curious way, with a literary-social club called the Ark that would come to have a profound effect felt to this day.

It was founded in 1835 by the two sons of Leonard Case Sr.— Leonard Jr. and William—in a little wooden building that had been their father's law office near Public Square. Most members were the second generation of the city's original New England power structure.

There was no constitution, bylaws or formal organization. Members got together and talked about similar interests, primarily natural science, although reading and discussion were high on their list. They gradually collected animal and bird specimens, and the rooms began to look like a museum. That suggested to them an ark, and the members became Arkites.

Truman Handy, founder of the Cleveland Mozart
Society. *(Cleveland Public Library)*

In 1839, a letter from Leonard Jr., then a student at Yale, to his brother William, suggested that the office was something more than a place of business. "Does the office continue to be the headquarters for loafers, as usual, or is it getting to be too notorious?" he asked.

A letter of William's in 1841 says, "I have a live rattlesnake to show for the amusement of the girls, who begin to think the old office a curiosity shop."

This happy band would be responsible over the next century for the natural science museum that eventually evolved into the Museum of Natural History, the Cleveland Library Association, Case Hall, Case Library, and Case School—in short, Case Institute.

Then there was banker-businessman Truman Handy who founded a choral group, the Cleveland Mozart Society, "for the promotion of musical science and the cultivation of a refined taste in its members, and in the community." The new monied magnates looked back to Europe for the art forms they most admired, and these would obviously be classical.

Cleveland was way behind the East Coast and Cincinnati when

it came to trying any local productions of fine arts, and it would be another generation before there was strong support for local artists. But when it came to lectures, the house would be packed when Horace Greeley, Horace Mann or Bayard Taylor come to town. Oratory was considered the height of fine arts.

The fabulous Jenny Lind, the "Swedish Nightingale," came to Kelley's Hall in November 1851, with the benefit of the usual publicity build-up from her manager, P.T. Barnum. Some 1,125 spectators paid $2 to $4 apiece to hear her sing "John Anderson My Jo."

When onlookers watching her through a skylight on the roof burst through the glass, creating a momentary panic, Lind immediately sang her famous "Bird Song," calming the audience.

The Plain Dealer critic said, "We thought we had known the resources of the song, but Jenny Lind turned up whole treasures of new wealth."

Her boss, old P.T. Barnum, put it best: "She was a woman who would have been adored if she had had the voice of a crow."

Oberlin-Wellington Rescue
Struck Blow against Slavery

How did early Clevelanders feel about the question of slavery?

Nobody was taking public opinion polls in those days, but probably the majority of northern Ohioans weren't particularly sympathetic to the slaves, and definitely detested most abolitionists.

As the country became increasingly divided, however, so did local opinion. There was an active Anti-Slavery Society in the country by the late 1830s. By 1841, Cleveland had become an important stop on the Underground Railway for slaves escaping through Ohio to Canada and freedom.

Prominent citizens risked arrest to secretly house desperate blacks; St. John's Episcopal Church on the West Side housed fugitives in its belfry, waiting for signals from boats to send the people out.

The southern slave-catchers congregated in Cleveland where they had a good chance of making slavery arrests under the fugitive slave laws of the day. The abolitionists had an arrangement with the Old Stone Church to ring its bell when a slave-catcher was spotted in the city.

In 1841 three slaves found in Buffalo were kidnapped and sent back to jail in Cleveland. Local abolitionist lawyers weren't allowed to represent them, but a nonabolitionist, Thomas Bolton, successfully defended them in the face of violent threats from an outraged public.

But it would be 1858 before Cleveland made history for its part in what would become known as the Oberlin-Wellington Rescue.

Oberlin College had about 1,200 students at that time, and the college had no color, sex, or religious barriers. This drew many runaway slaves, including John Price, who had escaped from slavery in Kentucky.

A slave-catcher decoyed him to Wellington, 9 miles away, to take him by train before the U.S. commissioner at Columbus. But students, professors and townspeople from Oberlin and Wellington surrounded the hotel where Price was being guarded. They managed to free Price, whose next stop would be Canada and freedom.

Thirty-seven men were indicted by the Cleveland U.S. attorney under the provisions of the detested Fugitive Slave Act; they were defended by four of the city's best attorneys, without fees. Their defense: an appeal to a higher law.

After the first defendant was found guilty and sentenced to 60 days in jail and fined $600, there was such an uproar at the judge's rulings that the rest of the defendants refused bail and voluntarily let themselves be jailed.

The martyrdom worked. Public meetings were conducted and there was a tremendous convention of opponents of the slave law in Cleveland on May 24, 1859. "Delegations came by trainload and wagonload. There were multitudes of bands and banners. A vast parade formed and marched by the prison yard cheering the martyrs."

St. John's Episcopal Church, considered to be the oldest church in the city, was one of the main stops in Northeast Ohio on the Underground Railroad. *(CSU)*

A large platform was built in Public Square so near to the high fence around the hall that speakers could harangue the crowd from either side. The prisoners wrote the newspapers, issued pamphlets; the railroads carried relations and friends to Cleveland at reduced rates.

The Lorain County grand jury indicted the four slave-catchers for violation of Ohio's kidnapping laws. The Cleveland prosecutor soon realized that the kidnappers were either going to stand trial and certainly be convicted, or allowed to leave the state and abandon the government's case against the rescuers. So, a deal was struck—slave-catchers and rescuers were all released. Clevelanders had a joyous celebration.

By January of 1861, public opinion had turned against slavery. When a posse of U.S. marshals forced their way into L.A. Benton's Prospect St. house and arrested a runaway slave girl named Lucy, a threatening crowd gathered—on her side this time. It took 150 armed men to bring her before the U.S. commissioner who reluctantly had to rule against her and for her Wheeling owner.

Prominent citizens offered her owner twice the slave's market value, but he took her back on a train under armed guard. She may have been the last slave returned to the South under the Fugitive Slave Law.

Two weeks later the shooting started at Fort Sumter and settled the matter of a "higher law" once and for all.

Journalists Not Shy in Early Newspaper Days

By the time The Plain Dealer's first edition hit the streets of Cleveland in January 1842, it had five competitors going after the population of 7,500—the Herald, the Morning Mercury, the Eagle-Eyed News Catcher, the Commercial Intelligencer, and the Gatherer.

In 1842, Cleveland's six newspapers engaged in gloves-off, partisan journalism. There was never any question about where they stood on any political or social issue. It made for interesting reading in the 19th century, when Cleveland's favorite entertainment was politics, and The Plain Dealer's owners, the Gray brothers, Joseph and Admiral, were Democrats with a capital "D."

Something of the Gray brothers' feisty nature comes through in their first editorial. In it, they explain why they changed the name of the paper they had purchased from The Advertiser to The Plain Dealer:

"We offer no apology for changing the name of this paper. . . . We think the good taste of our readers will sanction the modest selection we have made. Had we called it the Torpedo, timid ladies would never have touched it. Had we called it the Truth Teller, no one would believe a word in it! Had we called it the Thunder Dealer or Lightning Spitter it would have blown Uncle Sam's mail-bags sky-high. But our democracy and modesty suggest the only name that befits the occasion, 'The Plain Dealer.'"

Nineteenth century newspapers made no attempt to be objective, in news stories or editorials. For example, the editor of The Plain Dealer, Joseph W. Gray, was also the chairman of the Ohio delegation to the Democratic Convention in Baltimore in 1852.

The Democrats had so many strong candidates, and were so split by sectional rivalries, that after 34 ballots the delegates were deadlocked and thinking of possible dark-horse candidates.

The first choice was Ohio's Governor Reuben Wood, a Cleveland resident; in fact, all the governor would have needed at that point was his own Ohio delegation's votes to put him over the top. No

Joseph W. Gray founded The Plain Dealer with
his brother, Admiral Nelson Gray.
(Cleveland Public Library)

problem, right? Wrong! Editor Joseph Gray was marching to a different drummer, as usual, and refused to support Wood.

The convention went on to pick another dark horse, Franklin Pierce of New Hampshire, who went on to become president. Joseph Gray's stated reason for not backing his fellow townsman was that the governor was a "Hunker"—an ultra-conservative Democrat—a wing of the party that the editor detested.

Wood had to settle for a consulship in Chile; shortly thereafter, he retired to his estate on Ridge Rd., in what is now the Far West Side.

Joseph Gray, on the other hand, was named postmaster by the grateful president in 1853; but he got his comeuppance when President Lincoln appointed as his successor his arch-rival Edwin Cowles, editor of their great rival publication, the Cleveland Leader—full of committed Republicans! Cowles, vitriolic and flamboyant, had three great enemies: the Democratic Party, slavery, and the Catholic Church.

So, The Plain Dealer had a few unkind words to say about the new postmaster:

"To select so obnoxious an individual personally on the score of being a ruffian Republican is more than even Clevelanders can bear. The appointment of Cowles, personally unfit, simply because [he is] connected with a sheet owned and used by the irrepressibles to slaughter the conservatives and put down the liberal sentiments of the party looks so much like 'rule or ruin' that the masses are indignant.'

And later, warming up to the subject, ". . . one of the most base and infamous of creatures, who, wearing the garb of a human, has nearly all the elements of a demon. . . . If he not be his Satanic Majesty in person, he is worse still, being one of his dastardly and treacherous imps."

Wow! You have to admit that journalism was more fun in the days before libel laws!

Religious Commune Gave
Shaker Heights Its Birth

Shaker Heights has always figured prominently in Cleveland's history—in fact, in America's social history. It was one of the country's first planned suburban communities, and also one of the wealthiest. And it still gets attention from the national news media for the quality of its educational facilities. But it certainly didn't start out that way.

Shaker takes its name from the Shakers, the nickname for the religious sect called the United Society of the Second Coming of Christ. Rather than pronounce this mouthful, it was much simpler to name the group after its ritual dancing, in which members shook with religious frenzy, laughing and crying while they "labored mightily for the gift of love," as one Shaker sister put it.

When the founder of the sect, Mother Ann Lee, landed in New York from England in 1774, her eight followers believed she was the second coming of Christ. Members of her sect agreed to confess their sins, renounce marriage, give any children born to them to the group to raise, practice celibacy, donate their property to the society and live apart from the sinful world in their own communities.

It was hardly an attractive agenda by today's standards, but a tremendous religious revival swept across colonial America after 1780. Shaker communities were founded in seven states and in a little Ohio town north of Cincinnati called Lebanon. The group there named itself Union Village.

In 1821 a farmer named Ralph Russell, who lived in a log cabin near the present intersection of Shaker Blvd. and Lee Rd., visited Union Village and returned home ecstatic with his new-found religion—so much so that he proceeded to convert his many brothers and sisters into their own North Union community.

The community opened in March 1822, with "testimony" from several elders of the Lebanon parent community. Russell built more cabins near his for the expected converts, and on Sept. 20, the first public meeting was held to teach new members the sect's history and dances.

Since the Shakers had renounced marriage and practiced celibacy, they needed a steady stream of converts to survive. Well, the North Union group was having plenty of inspirational visions in the 1840s, and this aided in the recruiting. They set aside a grassy clearing surrounded by a circle of large, beautiful trees north of Shaker Blvd. in the Paxton Rd. area and called it the Holy Grove. (Perhaps the Druids of Stonehenge had something similar in mind).

Here in the Grove, sect members saw and heard strange things. One claimed to see "A band of angels, 24 in number, with gold trumpets which they were to sound to awake the children of the world." Another heard "the gift of a song in the Indian tongue to one of the children." Another said that "many made mighty testimonies against the flesh."

Men, women and children were separated from each other in large groups called families, which were presided over by elders and eldresses. When they all got together for worship in their meeting house, the religious brothers and sisters entered by different doors, dressed with Quaker simplicity, similarly believing in living their lives according to religious principles.

But there the resemblance ended, because a Shaker community was meant to be a "Colony of Heaven" where men and women lived apart from each other and a sinful world.

Otherworldly or not, the Shakers knew they needed money to live in this world, so they built a grist mill, stone quarry, sawmill, shops and barns where they made tubs, clothespins, brushes, pipes, furniture, silks and linens.

A Shaker flat corn broom—in fact, anything Shaker-made—was always the best quality and had a startlingly attractive simplicity; even their garden seed was famous. They built dams on Doan Brook that not only gave them the water power to operate a woolen mill, but also created one of the Shaker Lakes.

By 1837, the Shakers were doing so well financially and spiritually that they created a "Gathering Order"—a separate family "for the express purpose of gathering souls out in the world who are desirious of salvation and are willing to make the necessary sacrifice in order to obtain it."

But there was trouble coming to this "Valley of God's Pleasure," as the sect called its 1,400 acres. Young people didn't want to live this kind of an abstinent life. "Fifteen of our young people have gone to the world in less than two weeks," wrote one Shaker diarist. Another predicted, "Youth shall ever be our burden."

With a shortage of young muscle, expensive outside labor had to be hired, and this put the society in a losing financial position. Then there was the enmity of those around them, who detested this early socialistic society. At one point, armed raiders swept in on horseback and burned them out.

The Shakers rebuilt, but membership, which had gone from 89 in 1829 to a peak of 153 by 1860, went steadily downhill until the group disbanded in 1889.

A few stone gateposts and a tiny cemetery are all that's left of this gentle people, who dedicated themselves to a way of life based on honesty, hard work, and simplicity.

J.D. Rockefeller's Influence Extensive

Cleveland in 1850 was a picturesque small city with a population of 17,034. No less a visitor than an editor of the Cincinnati Gazette testified that "The town is clean, tasteful, elegant, and healthful; for vegetables, fruits and flowers it is preeminent—for groves, parks, trees and ornamental shrubs it is hardly surpassed by New Haven. . . . Her public and private schools are excellent; her medical college superior to any in the West, and the prevailing character of her society is educational, moral and religious. It is therefore, just the spot for the man of moderate income, to live and educate his family."

This pleasant scene was about to change rapidly as the Industrial Revolution and Civil War hit the city. Horse-drawn barges still floated on the Ohio Canal, schooners still sailed on Lake Erie, but the city's five railroads had driven the old, lumbering stagecoaches almost completely off the cobblestone streets.

Hotels were packed. The boom-town feel had started with the oil strike in western Pennsylvania in 1859. Cleveland began to cash in on it when the Atlantic & Great Western Railroad, with a line directly into the oil regions, completed its western terminus here, pounding final spikes in the day after Robert E. Lee retreated in July 1863 from Gettysburg.

There was now an efficient way to transport crude petroleum from the wells to the refineries. The railroad also linked Cleveland with the Eastern Seabord markets.

On Nov. 2, the railroad's first train, its shiny locomotive flying the flag, steamed into the city at a speedy 40 mph. The Board of Trade held a celebratory banquet with Gen. James Garfield, Amasa Stone, and other prominent local men as guests. But they probably didn't invite the cold-eyed, ruthless young man with the slit of a mouth whose oil shipments would shortly constitute the railroad's heaviest freight—and he almost certainly wouldn't have wasted his time by attending if they had.

By the time he was in his forties, John D. Rockefeller was one of the richest men in the country. *(CSU)*

This, of course, was the legendary John D. Rockefeller.

John D. died in 1937, not quite 98 years old, and "rich as Rockefeller" remains a byword for great wealth today. In his day, he was reviled and revered and no biographer, starting with the famous muckraker Ida Tarbell in 1901, up to the present, seems to have captured the whole man. Most agree that Rockefeller had complete and total control over his emotions—never, never, did he expose the inner self.

John's father, William Avery Rockefeller, was a peddler of patent medicines and miraculous medical cures operating as "Dr. Rockefeller" from a wagon for long periods out West, away from his New York state home. "The Doctor" was a pitchman, horse-trader, possibly a womanizer, but he valued education.

Thus after moving his family to Strongsville in 1853, he sent his two oldest sons, John and William, to Cleveland's only high school, Central High. John would meet his future wife, Laura Spelman, there, and another future prominent Clevelander, Mark Hanna. Both were 14 years old.

John D. clerked for a vegetable commission house in the Flats until he learned the business. Then he formed a partnership with Maurice Clark and started his own firm of Clark and Rockefeller, down in the Flats where there were already rolling mills, foundries, shipyards, shops, wholesale houses and noisy docks, using an advance he borrowed from his father for his end of the partnership capital.

John paid interest on this advance—and far from complaining, he admired his father's business sense: "He used to dicker with me and buy things from me. He taught me how to buy and sell."

The same year that Clark and Rockefeller went into business, 1859, a certain Col. Drake struck oil in Titusville, Pa., and the world would never be the same again. When the Civil War broke out in 1861, there were only two topics worth discussing in Cleveland— the war, and oil.

Clark and Rockefeller were doing well. When the war broke out, the partners saw their commissions grow as a result of handling oil shipments from the booming western Pennsylvania oilfields. John D. was very interested in oil—not in drilling, for there was too much risk in the production side; he wanted to refine it into that great new illuminant that everyone wanted, kerosene.

There were already 20 refineries along the Cuyahoga by 1863, covering it with a viscous scum, making the skies smokey with fires from gasoline, an unwanted by-product of distilling.

When the railroad tied Cleveland in with both the oil patch and Eastern markets with a direct line, John D. knew it was time to make his move; and that move would soon shake Cleveland and the world.

July 1863 saw the North turn back the Southern tide at Gettysburg. When Abraham Lincoln went there in November to dedicate the cemetery and deliver an address that would be long remembered, The Plain Dealer sent a reporter to the ceremonies. "The weather being fine," he said, "the program was carried out successfully."

Of President Lincoln's speech? Not a word!

Abe Lincoln Visits Cleveland

President-Elect's Pre-Inaugural Tour
Stirred the City

Cleveland was wild with excitement on Feb. 15, 1861; President-elect Abraham Lincoln was due in town the next afternoon on his way to the March 4 inaugural in Washington. Newspapers were playing it up so much that they elicited some snide comments from the Buffalo Courier about "putting on airs," and other social sins of the era.

Nobody from Cleveland really knew the lanky lawyer from Illinois whose reputation as "Honest Abe," had carried him to victory over better-known candidates at the Republican convention in Chicago in August 1860. Then, in November, he had gone on to take 60 percent of the Northern vote with a platform that was anti-slavery, but moderate enough to appeal to the lower tier of Northern states and win the presidency without Southern votes.

By the time Lincoln headed east for the inauguration, South Carolina, Alabama, Georgia, Florida, Texas, Mississippi and Louisiana had seceded from the Union. Fort Sumter in Charleston harbor was being blockaded by the rebel states and they were threatening war.

But Lincoln kept his future plans for dealing with the secession to himself, to the approval of the editor of the Cleveland Leader who felt that Lincoln had already committed himself to upholding constitutional government, with all that that implied toward the South, and compared this to the corrupt Buchanan administration—"no government at all," still sitting in Washington, doing absolutely nothing.

The crowds gathered all day on Feb. 16 at the Euclid Station depot. The sidewalks were lined for miles miles and doors, windows and yards were filled with spectators. A police and military escort waited, and when the whistle of the Pittsburgh train sounded, "the horses of the dragoons plunged and reared, men shouted, women screamed, and children crawled out miraculously unharmed from beneath the heels of the steeds."

A procession continued along Euclid Ave. made up of wagons, a miniature ship on wheels, 75 workmen from the Cuyahoga Steam Furnace Co., the men of the Forest City Tool Co., fire engine companies, City Council and others.

Signs said, "Welcome to the president of our beloved country"; "The Union, It Must Be Preserved." Men cheered, women waved handkerchiefs. At 5 p.m., the parade arrived at the famous Weddell House hotel where 20 rooms had been reserved for the president's party.

Later, Lincoln would give a speech from his balcony: "Fellow citizens of Cleveland and Ohio: We have come here upon a very inclement afternoon. We have marched for two miles through the rain and the mud.

"Your large numbers testify that you are in earnest about something. And what is that something? . . . I know that it is paid to something worth more than any one man, or any thousand, or any ten thousand men. A devotion to the Constitution, to the Union, and the Laws; to the perpetual liberty of the people of this country. . . . I think the present crisis is altogether an articial one. . . . What they do who seek to destroy the Union is altogether artificial. . . . Have they not the same Constitution and laws that they have always had, and have they always have been?

"I have not the strength, fellow citizens, to address you at great length, and I pray that you will excuse me; but rest assured that my thanks are as cordial and sincere for the efficient aid which you gave to the good cause is working for the good of the nation, as for the votes which you gave me last fall. . . .

"There is one feature that causes me great pleasure; and that is to learn that this reception is given, not alone by those with whom I chance to agree, politically, but by all parties. . . . this is as it should be . . . If we don't make common cause and save the good old ship, nobody will. . . .

"To all of you, then, who have done me the honor to participate in this cordial welcome, I return most sincerely my thanks, not for myself, but for Liberty, the Constitution, and Union. I bid you all an affectionate farewell."

Not the Gettysburg Address or the Second Inaugural, but warm, sincere, and from the heart—no spin doctors.

It would be four years later, in April 1865, before Abraham Lincoln would return to Cleveland in his funeral train, on the way to Springfield, Ill., his burial place.

41st Ohio's Heroic Civil War Role

The 41st Ohio Infantry regiment was a typical Civil War regiment of about 1,000 men from Cuyahoga County, including 400 from Cleveland. It was formed in August 1861, and in November began training at Camp Dennison. A month later, the regiment moved to Camp Wickliffe, 60 miles from Louisville, Ky., where it remained for the winter.

The regiment's Col. William Hazen was placed in command of an entire brigade, which consisted of the 41st, plus two Indiana regiments and one from Kentucky. By Feb. 1, 1862, the brigade was on its way down the Ohio River and up the Cumberland to Nashville. March 17, with the bands playing "St. Patrick's Day," the brigade marched with Gen. Don Carlos Buell's army towards a place on the Tennessee River called Pittsburg Landing where it was to combine with another army under the command of a newly famous general, U.S. Grant, for a joint attack on a large Confederate army at Corinth, Miss.

The 41st Ohio was down to 450 men. The record doesn't show whether this was due to sickness or part of the regiment being left behind in Nashville. When the brigade arrived late afternoon of April 6 on the bank of the Tennessee River opposite Pittsburg Landing, it was almost deafened by the thunderous sounds of battle.

The troops were ferried across the river where they ran into panicked, beaten stragglers. The untried Ohio boys must have been a little panicked themselves when they heard the stragglers: "You'll catch it on the hill," said one; "I am the only man left in my company," declared another.

The brigade pressed on, took up its assigned position and lay all night in a driving rain listening to the wounded crying out in the woods around them. The next day, in the midst of heavy artillery fire, the rebels came charging out of the brush yelling, "Bull Run!" "Bull Run!" The brigade stood and fought, broke the attack, counterattacked and captured the rebel position. When no support came up, the brigade had to retreat to its original lines.

In its first battle, the 41st Ohio had lost 141 killed and wounded of its 450 men. More than 20,000 of the Blue and Gray were killed or wounded in this first great Civil War slaughter. The North named the battle site after a little church nearby—Shiloh.

By September 1863, Union Gen. William "Old Rosy" Rosecrans had moved his army from Chattanooga across the Tennessee state line to a little creek in north Georgia called Chickamauga, where he ran headlong into Gen. Braxton Bragg's Confederate army. During the battle the Union side did very well until, through a mistaken order, a regiment was withdrawn from the center of its line leaving a large gap. The Southerners quickly poured through the opening, routing thousands of the bluecoats. It looked like the Union army was going to be destroyed.

But Ohio's veteran 41st Infantry didn't panic. On the morning of Sept. 19, the Ohioans had their skirmish line out front when they ran into the rebels storming through the Union lines. Their lieutenant yelled, "Lie down!" The skirmishers crawled back on their hands and knees while the regiment fired volleys over their heads into the Confederate ranks. Two Southern bayonet charges were stopped within 30 feet of the regimental lines.

The rebels, however, worked their way around the regiment's position and for the first and only time in their military history, members of the 41st turned and ran. When they joined the other three regiments in their brigade, they made a successful stand.

All that night the men rolled logs into a barricade. The next morning the Southerners attacked again and again, but the brigade hurled them back with heavy losses. Later that afternoon, the brigade retreated under heavy fire to join with the only part of the Union army that was still fighting—and here the men fought again, this time as the rear guard that saved the Union army at the Battle of Chickamauga. The next evening the remnants of the 41st arrived safely back in Chattanooga.

By February of 1864, the regiment was freezing in eastern Tennessee. It now consisted of 188 men, and most of these had been wounded at least once. With their three-year enlistments due to expire, the government requested they re-enlist for three more years. One hundred and eighty said yes, and would march with Gen. William Tecumseh Sherman to Atlanta.

Cleveland Grays, Born to Parade, Lived, Died In War

The Cleveland Grays were a private military company formed in 1837 with 118 men from Cleveland's best families. They were named after their gray uniforms and they did their drilling in Public Square.

While they were formed to assist the local constabulary and provide army reserves in times of war, basically, they drilled to show off to their girlfriends. An old sketch shows them marching in ruler-straight lines with their officers in front, preceded by drummer boys.

The Grays took part in every notable social, civic or political event for the next 25 years. When local Whigs dedicated a log cabin for Gen. William Henry Harrison's presidential campaign, the Grays led the parade across town; they met the candidate himself later that year at the docks and marched him to his Public Square hotel. Ex-President Martin Van Buren got Grays' "treatment" in 1842, when he came to town.

In September 1860, 100,000 people jammed into Public Square for the dedication of the Oliver Hazard Perry monument. There were speeches, cannons booming, fireworks, a mock Battle of Lake Erie on the lake—and the Cleveland Grays marching.

But the crowning event came on Feb. 15, 1861, when President-elect Abraham Lincoln arrived in Cleveland at the Euclid St. railroad station. The Grays marched in perfect precision as church bells rang, factory whistles shrieked and the crowds cheered themselves hoarse. The next morning, the Grays conducted the presidential party to the Union Depot where Lincoln would go on to his March inauguration.

Two months later, in answer to Lincoln's call for troops, the Grays became Company D of Ohio's 1st Infantry regiment; 60 hours later, they were on their way to Washington. When rebels fired into the train in Virginia, the regiment fought them off with minor losses.

But the days of parades and cheering crowds were over. The

Cleveland Grays marching in Public Square, 1831. *(CSU)*

Cleveland Grays would now march right into the storm and blood of the Civil War. And they took a terrible beating. There were about 15,600 men available of which 10,000 enlisted; 1,700 died in battle or of disease, or in prisoner-of-war camps. Another 2,000 were wounded so badly that they were crippled for life.

A look at the roster of the 7th Infantry, a typical Cuyahoga County regiment, gives you the cold, hard facts of what could happen to these local men from the time they enlisted on June 19, 1861, till the survivors were mustered out in May, 1865. For example:

- Townley Gillet, promoted to corporal, was killed at Port Republic, Va., on June 8, 1862, in one of the hundreds of clashes that took place in the Shenandoah Valley.
- Leonard Wacker was reported missing after the Battle of Cedar Mountain, Aug. 9, 1862. Did he ever come back? Is he buried in an unmarked grave?
- Abraham Ginter died at Alexandria, Va., from wounds received in that same battle.
- Michael McCaune died of accidental wounds on Nov. 8, 1861, one week after he enlisted.
- Evan Evans and Andrew Scovill were taken prisoner on Aug. 26, 1862, at Cross Lanes, Va., an engagement in which the 7th Infantry lost heavily; they were paroled and exchanged, but never rejoined their regiment.

The longest list is of those "discharged for disability." Minus arms, legs, eyes? Probably. Also probably, some so horribly disfigured that they would spend the rest of their lives in a veterans hospital or in a darkened room where people wouldn't be shocked at the sight of their faces.

The famous battle of Chancellorsville took a heavy toll in May, 1863. Some more died on the way south from Tennessee with Gen. William T. Sherman in November 1863, on his way to Atlanta.

There's nothing from that date on until May, 1865, when the survivors were mustered out in Public Square; sun-burned men, some bearded, in baggy pants—and, a look in their eyes that comes through even in the grainy, old, black-and-white photos—a look that wasn't there when they left Cleveland four years earlier.

The Grays erected their armory on Bolivar Rd. in 1893, a facility on the National Register of Historic Places, and went on to serve the country in World Wars I and II. They continue in their historical social function, marching in parades and honoring military tradition, to this day.

Loose-Lipped Lincoln Haters Mobbed

Most Clevelanders were grief-stricken at the news of Abraham Lincoln's assassination on April 14, 1865, but not all; those who hated the president were delighted, and they talked—to anyone at hand that terrible day.

Here's what the Cleveland Leader had to say: "Some villians are fools—so great fools that they parade their villainy before the world. Certain visitors in Cleveland were crazy enough to express their joy at the murder of the President, and received therefore some very rough treatment.

"J.J. Husband, the well known architect, was in high glee after the news. remarking to one man, 'You have had your day of rejoicing, now I have mine,' to another, 'This is a good day for me,' and to a third, 'Lincoln's death is a damned small loss.' It seems that afterwards he became sensible of the danger that he had incurred by these remarks, for he came sneaking back to the newspaper offices to deny that he had made them."

A mob ran Husband from his office to the roof, caught him, threw him through a skylight into his office, and kicked him down the stairs. "The mob would perhaps have pounded him to death had he not been rescued by prominent citizens. Locked in a courthouse room, he broke free, and, we understand, has since left town. He can never show his face in Cleveland again. His name has already been chipped from the place on the Court House where it was cut as the architect. . . .

"Other men of Southern sympathies knew enough to keep closely at home, Saturday. Cleveland is an unhealthy place for rebels."

Across the North, there was a tremendous outpouring of grief—the tragedy following on the heels of victory in the bloody, four-year war being almost too much for people to grasp. The seven-car funeral train bearing the president's body set out on April 21 on a 1,700 mile journey retracing the stops the president-elect had made four years earlier, on the way to his first inauguration.

The Lincoln funeral train made a stop in Cleveland's public square, giving cause for some to mourn and others to rejoice. *(Cleveland Public Library)*

There were stops in New York, where a crowd of 100,000 mourners accompanied the cortege through the streets; Philadelphia, and then Baltimore. In Lancaster, Pa., a tired old man in a carriage watched from the edge of the crowd as the train passed— James Buchanan, Lincoln's predecessor. Finally, it was Cleveland's turn.

There, the Committee on Location of Remains had decided no available building would accommodate the crowds, so the Committee on Arrangements had a pagoda put up in the city park (Public Square), with open sides through which two columns could pass the coffin.

A high bank above the Lake Erie shore was jammed with people as the train drew into the Union Depot. From there another engine took it to the Euclid St. station, and it was noted: "As the train came up the Lake Shore track, a very beautiful incident took place. Miss Fields of Wilson St., had erected an arch of evergreens on the bank of the lake near the track, and as the train passed appeared in the arch as the Goddess of Liberty in mourning."

Maj. Gen. Joseph "Fighting Joe" Hooker was in charge of the

military escorting the hearse, which was drawn by six white horses wearing crepe rosettes and silver stars.

A procession of more than 6,000 people moved along Euclid St. to the park, as a slow rain began to fall. A burial service was read over the coffin; 9,000 an hour passed the coffin the first hours, growing ever larger till by park closing at 10 p.m. many, many thousands from northern Ohio, Detroit, and western Pennsylvania towns had shuffled by.

Later, with the wind driving torrents of rain, a night procession escorted the hearse through crowded streets to the depot. The train continued its westward journey to Springfield, Ill., past little groups of men and women at every crossroads standing by bonfires, their tears mixing with the rain, as Abraham Lincoln rode into enduring American legend.

Humorist Ward Started With PD

It was said that the only person who could make Abraham Lincoln laugh during the Civil War years was the famous American humorist Artemus Ward. The president kept a book of his witticisms by his side and would read parts of it to his unappreciative Cabinet. No matter: The important thing was that Abraham Lincoln would roar with laughter, his safety valve during those terrible years.

Ward's real name was Charles Farrar Brown, and he made his worldwide reputation in Cleveland writing for The Plain Dealer. Editor Charles Gray hired him in 1857 when he was 23. He had been knocking around as a tramp printer and occasional writer.

He had a pleasant effect on people when they met him. As one associate wrote, according to author George Condon, "His eyes were blue-gray, with a twinkle in them; his mouth seemed so given to a merry laugh, so much in motion, that it was difficult to describe, so we let it pass. . . . When we were introduced . . . he gave his leg a smart slap, arose and shook hands with me and said he was glad to meet me. I believed him for he looked glad all the time.

"He laughed as he sat at his table writing, and when he had written a thing that had pleased him he would slap his leg and laugh. . . . "

Brown began writing a column of hilarious letters addressed to himself from the mythical proprietor of a traveling circus in Pittsburgh, whom he called Artemus Ward. By 1860, every newspaper in the country was reprinting his Plain Dealer columns.

But humorist Brown felt that he was stuck in a rut with his $10 per week earnings; for this money he was also expected to be a reporter and a critic. Maybe this was what made him grumpy when he reviewed a lecture that Ralph Waldo Emerson gave in Cleveland in January 1859: "He [Emerson] is a man of massive intellect, but his lecture last night was rather a sleepy affair. For our part . . . we had quite as lief see a perpendicular coffin behind a lecture desk as Emerson. The one would amuse as much as the other."

When New York's Vanity Fair offered him a deal if he would give

In 1858 humorist Charles Farrar Brown began using the pseudonym Artemus Ward in The Plain Dealer. *(Cleveland Public Library)*

them first crack at his copy, he hastily accepted. But Gray wasn't amused, and didn't get any happier when Brown wanted $100 per month to stay with The Plain Dealer on an exclusive basis. So, they agreed to part company.

Charles Farrar Brown wrote his own farewell: "The undersigned closes his connection with The Plain Dealer with this evening's issue. During the three years that he has contributed to these columns he has endeavored to impart a cheerful spirit to them. He believes it is far better to stay in the Sunshine while we may, inasmuch as the Shadow must of its own accord come only too soon. . . . The undersigned may be permitted to flatter himself that he has some friends among the readers of this newspaper. Charles F. Brown."

Vanity Fair began publishing Charles F. Brown, (alias Artemus Ward), after the humorist left The Plain Dealer in 1860. Brown did so well that he published a book of his witticisms that sold 40,000 copies—a terrific sale for those times (and not bad today)!

He apparently continued to have Cleveland on his mind. This is what he had to say on the subject of Euclid St. (now Euclid Ave.): "A justly celebrated thoroughfare. Some folks go so far as to say it puts it all over the well known Unter der Sauerkraut in Berlin and the equally well known Rue de Boolfrog in Paree, France.

"Entering by way of the Public Square, and showing a certificate of high moral character, the visitor, after carefully wiping his feet on the welcome mat, is permitted to roam the sacred highway free of charge. The houses are on both sides of the street and seem large as well as commodious. They are covered with tin roofs and paint and mortgages, and present a truly distangy appearance.

"All the owners of Euclid Street homes employ hired girls and are patrons of the arts. A musical was held at one of these palatial homes the other day with singing. The soprano and the contralto were beautiful singers. The tenor has as fine a tenor voice as ever brought a bucket of water from a second-story window, and the basso sang so low that his voice at times sounded like the rumble in the tummy of a colicky whale!"

He became an international favorite on the lecture circuit, particularly with the English. As biographer Stephen Lealcock, said, "The English seem to have been delighted in the sheer 'cussedness' of the new American humor . . . and they treated him not as a comic entertainer, but as a comic genius."

In March 1867, at the height of his fame, Brown lay dying of tuberculosis, in Southampton. He started to write: "Some 12 years ago, I occupied the position [or the position occupied me] of city editor of a journal in Cleveland, Ohio. This journal—the Plain Dealer—was issued afternoons. . . . "

The pencil fell from his hand. Charles Farrar Brown—Artemus Ward—was dead.

He was 33 years old.

And Now Pitching . . . A Fan

In this day of multimillionaire baseball owners, players, agents and TV network contracts, let's turn the pages back 125 years to a more gentle time, to Cleveland's first professional baseball team, the Forest Citys.

There were about 2,000 excited fans gathered at Case Commons on June 2, 1869, to see their brand-new team play the great Cincinnati Red Stockings. A lot of these spectators would have been Civil War vets who had learned the game in army camps. Many would have been men who had put in 10-hour, six-day workweeks in the foundries, oil refineries and shipyards that lined the Cuyahoga Valley. They needed a day off even if that meant spending 25 cents to stand, or 50 cents to view the game from a carriage.

Playing baseball for money, though, wasn't quite socially acceptable. On opening day, four of the nine players wouldn't even take any money; men like L.C. Hanna, brother of Mark Hanna, who would become a U.S. senator. Star catcher Jim "Deacon" White was paid $75 a month, and the other four pros, $65 per month.

The big, bad Red Stockings, who hadn't lost a game all year, arrived in their private carriage from the luxurious Weddell House.

Would the Forest Citys, in their first game, do the unbelievable? No way! Score: Red Stockings 25, Cleveland, 6. But one year later, in 1870, the Forest Citys beat the Brooklyn Atlantics, 132-1, good for 180 bases, a record that stands to this day.

Now fast-forward to 1895, when the Cleveland Spiders beat Baltimore in the National League's Temple Cup, the World Series of the day. The heady feeling didn't last long—three years later the Spiders had slipped to fifth place and fan interest waned.

Owner Frank Robison, the street railway magnate who also owned League Park, was infuriated by the drop in attendance. He bought the St. Louis franchise and moved his star players, Cy Young, Jesse Burkett, "Chief" Zimmer and manager/player "Patsy" Tebeau, among others, to St. Louis. Any player that couldn't make it there was sent to Cleveland.

Fans line up for tickets outside League Park in 1940. *(CSU)*

The Cleveland fans promptly dubbed the team, "The Misfits," and stayed away in droves. By 1899, only 500 showed up for the opening day doubleheader.

After playing 27 games in League Park, Robison decided after July 1 the team would not play any more home games there; they would play in nearby cities.

This brought results all right—perhaps the worst professional baseball team of all time; it won 20 and lost 134 games that season.

In 1900, the National League cut its membership to eight teams, and "The Misfits" was one of the four teams dropped.

But a couple of businessmen, Charlie Somers and Jack Kilfoyle, with more money than baseball sense, joined the new American League and began to raid the National League teams for talent. Public pressure forced Frank Robison to lease League Park to the new "Bronchos," and they promptly headed for the cellar, lost 13 of their first 17 games. They sorely lacked pitching depth.

But according to author Franklin Lewis:

The desperate manager of the Bronchos, Bill Armour, asked for volunteer semipro and amateur pitchers. One day, one of them, a man named Otto Hess, beat the Washington Senators in his first start. But the next day, the Bronchos were facing Connie Mack's great Philadelphia Athletics, with the legendary Rube Waddell pitching, and Armour had nobody ready to face him.

Arriving at the field, Armour took a tip from a ticket-taker, grabbed a spectator out of the bleachers named Charlie Smith, who pitched around town for the Cleveland Wheel Club, borrowed a pair of spike shoes, put him in a uniform, and Charlie Smith won 5-4 when the Bronchos got a ninth inning single from player/manager 'Nap' Lajoie.

Look, we're not trying to tell Dick Jacobs how to run his business, but maybe—just maybe—up in those Jacobs Field stands. . . . !

Prosperity Brought Flow of Immigrants

You would think that after the Civil War, one of the most destructive in history, the country would have been plunged into a terrible depression. And the South was. But to the North, the war brought prosperity, a sense of power and exuberant energy.

Population and wealth increased even during the war years with its manpower shortage. Oil production, iron ore output, coal, railroad mileage, pig iron—all made astronomical leaps—along with high taxes, debt and inflation.

By 1870, per capita wealth had doubled. The number of manufacturing plants had increased by 80 percent and those plants—in Chicago, St. Louis, Pittsburgh, Detroit, San Francisco—needed more workers. Even during the war, more than 800,000 immigrants poured into the country. Cleveland's population went from 43,414 in 1860, to 92,829 in 1870, and a decade later would be over 160,000.

The city had gotten its share of war orders and then some. The foundries, rolling mills, and shipyards had boomed; orders for uniforms had started the textile industry. Chemical plants were built to supply sulfuric acid to Cleveland's many oil refineries. And thousands of Irish and German immigrants continued to pour in to fill those smoky, dirty jobs.

By 1866, the city's five railroads had joined in building a new Union depot at the foot of what is now W. 9th St., and it was here, after 1870, that Czechs and Slovaks, Poles, Slovenes, Russian Jews, Serbs, Greeks and Italians arrived from eastern Europe. Many of the Czechs went into skilled trades such as machine-tool making, carpentry, masonry, baking and brewing; the Slovaks and Poles tended toward the heavy-lifting jobs.

Thousands of girls were employed in cigar and candy plants, cloak-and-suit factories, working as teachers, clerks, laundresses, seamstresses and house servants. Paint, varnish and sewing-machine industries would come along a few years later.

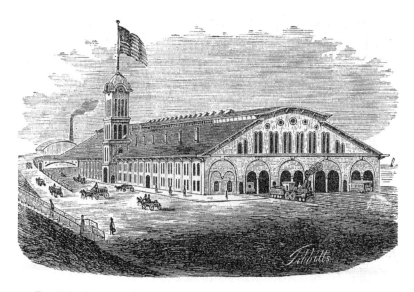

The Union Passenger Depot was the last stop for many immigrants who made Cleveland their home. *(CSU)*

Some of the European immigrants were brought over by employers recruiting for cheap labor, emptying whole villages; others, by paternalistic owners such as Theodor Kundtz. Once a penniless immigrant Kundtz brought thousands of poor Hungarians over to work in his plants that made the wood cabinets for the White Sewing Machine Co.; "Kundtz" would be printed on a slip pinned to the new arrival's shirt.

The immigrants clustered in their own neighborhoods, crowding into tar-paper shacks and boardinghouses, speaking only Polish in Warszawa, Slovakian in the Haymarket District south of Public Square; Irish brogue on the near West Side and Whiskey Island, Yiddish on Scovill Avenue between E. 30th and E. 70th streets, where thousands of Russian Jews moved.

There were scores of ethnic language newspapers, beer halls, social clubs, churches. And there was poverty and disease: typhoid and cholera were often fatal. Unsanitary conditions the norm. It was a rare family that hadn't lost one or more children at an early age. Soup kitchens and orphanages became part of the scene.

For most of the newcomers, Cleveland was the fabled American melting-pot, but not all of them liked this dog-eat-dog life. Perhaps one-third of them came, saw, and went back to Europe with their savings, put off by this dirty, brawling city.

Historians tell of this letter from a new arrival: "We walked along Broadway . . . we branched off around the Rockefeller barrel works . . . we took our stand before a gate where about 20 people were already waiting. They all looked longingly toward the closed gates . . . At last the gates were opened . . . a clerk came, chose about 4 men and waved the rest of us away.

"Everything in the vicinity reeked of oil so that it was difficult to breathe. We walked farther along the valley, and crossed a wooden bridge over a river whose like I had never seen in all my life; yellow-ish rings of oil circled on its surface, like grease on soup; the water was yellowish, thick, full of clay, stinking of oil and sewage. The water heaped rotting wood on both banks of the river; everything was dirty and neglected. I didn't try and hide from my friend the fact that I was disappointed by this view of an American river. . . . [My friend] gave me some advice: 'My boy, you must forget Bohemia; you're in America now.'

And how did the older Clevelanders, the English, Scotch, Welsh, respond to these newcomers? Why, that old American way: They began to move to the suburbs.

Industrial Age
Both Boon, Bane to City

Abraham Lincoln had declared in 1859, "If any continue through life in the condition of the hired laborer, it is not the fault of the system, but because of either a dependent nature . . . or improvidence, folly, or singular misfortune."

Six years later, Abraham Lincoln was gone and so also was the idea that working for someone else was only a temporary condition on the way up the economic ladder. Seven out of ten laborers now worked for 10 cents an hour in shop conditions that were often unsafe and unsanitary.

While the Civil War had brought higher wages to working men and women and wages paid in paper dollars for the first time in the country's history, the greenbacks fluctuated wildly in price. The huge Northern armies created a labor shortage, helping spur inflation that ran 80 percent in four years of warfare.

And something else had changed by the war's end: returning vets went back to their jobs to find that their old employers had grown immensely big and successful. The boss couldn't know all of his workers' names or take a personal interest in their lives anymore. How could Henry Chisholm, president of the Cleveland Rolling Mill Co., possibly know all of his 5,000 employees, now busily turning out steel in their new Bessemer furnaces?

And in this new "Industrial Age," if you objected to the usual 60-hour week, there were immigrants pouring into the city by the thousands to take your place. Many workers, feeling that they were isolated and helpless and losing control of their lives, turned increasingly to unions.

Cleveland had always had local skilled trade unions. Now, these united into national unions such as typographers, carpenters, blacksmiths, iron molders and hat-finishers, and some of the biggest were headquartered here.

The Brotherhood of Locomotive Engineers made Cleveland their home in 1873; this was one of the key unions in the giant rail-

Henry Chisholm's steel company, Cleveland Rolling Mill, helped usher in a new age of Northeast Ohio manufacturing. *(Cleveland Public Library)*

road industry. The Knights of Labor, the biggest of the 32 national unions, believed in a coalition of farmers, workingmen and small business, and it was because of them that the first Farmer-Labor representatives met in Cleveland in 1875.

Their leaders were political and social reformers who couldn't conceive of a permanent wage-earning class; most relied on political education and action. Strikes were only a last resort.

Any idea of the unity of business and labor was forgotten when an economic panic in 1873 hit the country and led to a flat-out battle between the two sides for a share of the decreasing pie. Cleveland, along with the rest of the country, suffered.

Hundreds of local businesses folded, throwing thousands out of work. Railroads, desperate for traffic, cut rates and wages. Standard Oil cut wages to an average of 56 cents a day. Labor leaders who called for strikes were promptly fired, and they and their followers were quickly replaced by the immigrants. When the cooper's union walked out taking other locals with them, the strike turned violent. Newspapers and local sentiment went against the strikers, and the strike collapsed.

When an unauthorized railroad strike broke out in Martinsburg, W.Va., in 1877, after the Baltimore and Ohio Rail Road cut wages, the militia had to be called in. The strike spread to Philadelphia, and then Pittsburgh, where the night sky was lit up with the glare of a burning roundhouse.

Cleveland railroaders walked out on July 23, 1877, after pledging themselves, according to historian William G. Rose, to "abstain from all intoxicating liquors during the trouble," and promising to protect all property belonging to the railroad. But the city was still against them: Diplomat John Hay wrote angrily about "the rebellion of foreign workmen. The town is full of thieves and tramps waiting and hoping for a riot."

In 1882, the Cleveland Rolling Mills Co. locked out its skilled union workers, mostly English, Scots and Welsh, when they struck, replacing them with unskilled Polish immigrants. Some were given revolvers to protect themselves, leading to more bloody clashes.

Within three years, the despised foreign strike-breakers, rejected by the steelworkers union on religious and ethnic grounds, united in the face of successive wage cuts to use stones, clubs and those same guns against their employers. In the end, nothing was really resolved: the wage cuts were restored, but the strikers weren't re-hired.

Cleveland in the late 19th century was beginning to learn the downside of the brave, new Industrial Age.

Civil War Liberated Women, Too

In pre-Civil War Cleveland, men had placed middle-class women on a pedestal of moral supremacy, and that was where they were supposed to stay. As for economic and political rights, forget it.

Women who wanted to get out of their assigned niche of home and family could get involved with their communities in only a few ways: anti-slavery work, temperance, teaching (at half the salary of males), and charities—always through their churches. All that would change during and after the war.

During most of the 1800s, working women—Irish, German, Bohemian—had even more limited opportunities than women of means. They could become house servants, seamstresses, washerwomen, do sewing, or occasionally scrape up enough savings to open a small retail business, according to women's historian Marian Morton.

And of course, in a hustling lake town full of sailors, there was prostitution, about which the male church ministers fulminated and fumed while their female members very practically went down to the Flats to offer charitable assistance.

In 1851, The Cleveland Plain Dealer snickered at the Cleveland feminists who had been inspired by the first Women's Rights Convention at Seneca Falls, N.Y., three years earlier:

"Imagine a Whig husband and a Democratic wife, a free-soil uncle and a hunker aunt, a liberty party cousin, a colonization nephew, a slave-holding niece and 3 blooming daughters who have gone over bodice and bustle to the terrified democracy and for the first time in their lives will vote in pink muslin at the next election! Imagine this group gathered around the same table, tea and muffins, graced by Mr. Wm. Lloyd Garison . . . looking in at the window! How long would a well-built house probably stand, thus divided against itself?"

The women of Cleveland were not amused; while the country was being torn apart in debates over slavery and states' rights, none of the men seemed at all concerned over the fact that women

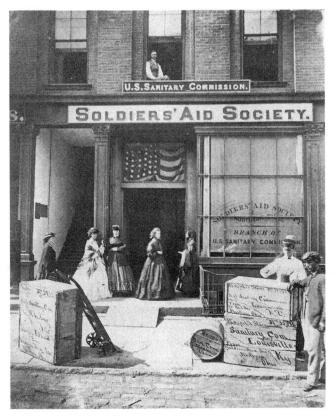

This Soldiers' Aid Society center on Bank St. (now W. 6th St.)
provided medical services and support to Civil War soldiers.
(Western Reserve Historical Society)

couldn't vote and had very little in the way of legal rights. It was typical of the outlook of the times that when a private boarding school for young ladies called the Cleveland Female Seminary opened in 1854, the entire board of directors and the principal were all prominent male civic leaders. Only the vice principal and teachers were women. That vice principal, Linda Thayer Guilford, would become the city's leading female educator.

The Civil War would begin a sea-change for American women. Only eight days after the first shots were fired at Fort Sumter, Cleveland women, under the leadership of Mrs. Rebecca Rouse, formed the Ladies Aid Society on April 20, 1861. The society took over the job of supplying families of poor soldiers with food and clothing, often going door-to-door to collect anything they could.

They were so successful that they later opened scores of branches and took the name of the Soldiers Aid Society of Northern Ohio, which later became part of the U.S. Sanitary Commission. The local women not only ran this organization, but took care of nursing, sanitation, feeding and clothing in the local camps and hospitals.

They raised almost $1 million during the war years, spending it entirely on the soldiers and their needy families.

With the war over and the Industrial Age in full swing, thousands of immigrant women from southeastern Europe were added to the pre-war mix of working women, many desperately poor and uneducated, crowding into tenements and boarding houses. This led to the swamping of the small charitable organizations and their replacement with major social welfare institutions, now backed not only by all church denominations, but by husbands and fathers, the newly rich industrial barons.

The Women's Christian Association was established here in 1868, the national Woman's Christian Temperance Union in 1874, soon to be the largest women's organization in the country. A Catholic nursing order opened the city's first permanent general hospital, St. Vincent Charity Hospital, in 1865. Homes for the aged, orphanages, schools opened.

But by the 1880s, even the major church social welfare organizations would be overwhelmed, and Cleveland women would have to put feminine rights on hold while they met these challenges.

Euclid Ave. Once Home to Rich, Famous

Cleveland had a whole new set of millionaires created by the Civil War, and their money was burning a hole in their pockets.

One of the best ways to show off their new wealth was to build palatial homes on Euclid Ave., preferably on the elite north side of the street. Those who preferred the West Side of town headed to Franklin Circle.

Most of the homes were a sort of American pseudo-Gothic, with ostentatious ornamentation; florid, showy, saying just what their successful owners wanted to procalim: "Hey, look at me! I've made it big!"

There were spires and battlements, gables and buttresses, stained glass windows and gargoyles, jigsaw scrollwork, ornate fireplaces and mantles, elaborate hangings, bric-a-brac galore.

American architectural taste had gone downhill since the early Greek Revival days of Thomas Jefferson and Benjamin Latrobe. Architectural critic Lewis Mumford said, "Architectural anarchy had reached a point at which disorder had resulted almost in physical brutality, and ugliness conducted a constant assault and battery wherever one turned one's eye. When one beholds some of the famous buildings of the period, one must charitably assume that they were built for the blind, for a generation that dwelt in darkness."

But Cleveland citizens didn't look at it that way, and they proudly showed off their "Millionaire's Row."

For example, there was Jeptha Wade's stone mansion on the northwest corner of Euclid and Case (E. 40th St.). He was the Western Union Telegraph Co. tycoon. His son's mansion adjoined his.

Wade had three dozen stone pillars costing $1,000 each supporting his gates; coachmen and gardeners had cottages on the grounds. For neighbors he had Charles Otis, the father of the

The Mather Mansion was one of many palatial estates that dotted
"Millionaires' Row" on Euclid Avenue. *(CSU)*

American Steel & Wire Co., and T.S. Beckwith, the master dry-goods retailer.

Even more sumptuous homes were built by Amasa Stone, W.J. Boardman, Samuel Mather, Stillman Witt, and others. The Sylvester Everett mansion had a porte-cochere that could fit a cavalry troop.

Lawns were so big that the ladies soon took up the new game of lawn tennis right in their front yards; winters you just put on the old buffalo robes and sleigh-raced with your neighbors through the thick, white snow from Case to Erie while thousands lined the route to cheer you on.

Even John D. Rockefeller, a man who studiously avoided a fun-loving social life, raced his own stable of horses from his home on the southwest corner of Case and Euclid.

There were bike races too, local clubs competing with their 5-foot-high front wheels and tiny rear wheels, sometimes at night, by gaslight. No noisy trolleys were allowed to interfere with the fun; they had long ago been routed south to Prospect.

Business, political, or social connections with Eastern society or best of all, European nobility, would inevitably be written up in one of the city's six newspapers.

Famous lecturers talked about this street in other countries, placing it on a par with St. Petersburg's Nevsky Prospect and Paris' boulevards for grandeur, according to Cleveland historian W.G. Rose.

Even Zanesville, Ohio, chipped in with an editorial that was reprinted in the May 27, 1868, Herald: "The fine architectural taste of the mansions which wealth has spared no pains in perfecting, the extensive grounds, the velvet green lawns, rare flowers and plants, the fountains that adorn each residence, many of them costing their owners over $100,000 before completion, are alone worth a trip to the lake to see."

Some people, of course, like The Plain Dealer humorist Artemus Ward, would make fun of them; others would point out that all that money had been spent on empty, ostentatious, neo-Gothic monstrosities that reflected their owners' lack of good taste.

By about the turn of the century, the street that had once been an Indian trail, and then the coach road to Buffalo, had turned into two miles of mansions, running out to Willson Ave. (E. 55th St.).

But the city was on the move. Eventually, the new immigrants would begin to push out east and west. Commercial and manufacturing buildings, used-car lots and fast-food restaurants would replace the mansions as their owners fled to the suburbs. Later, the immigrants themselves would seek those same suburbs.

The sound of the wrecker's ball would replace the sound of laughter from people on sleighs. No longer would there be the smell of summer flowers from wide, green lawns, nor the smell of money in the air on old Euclid Ave.

Bankrolling Higher Learning

Philanthropists' Feud Led to Founding of Two Schools

On a bitter, cold February day in 1851, a brightly polished new locomotive pulled into Cleveland packed with passengers from Columbus and Cincinnati to celebrate the completion of the city's first railroad, the Cleveland-Columbus-Cincinnati Co.

Among the officials who greeted the out-of-towners on the courthouse steps were the mayor, William Case, and the superintendent of the railroad, Amasa Stone, who not only had stock in the line, but a salary of $4,000 a year to run it.

These two were to clash in later years, and their mutual dislike and competitiveness would strongly affect higher education in Cleveland.

The famous and accomplished Case family: father, Leonard, and sons, Leonard Jr., and William, were unquestionably the first big names in 19th century Cleveland education, starting with the Cleveland Medical College in 1843. They also made several tries to create a Cleveland university, but came up short in the money department each time.

When Leonard Case Jr. died in 1880, he accomplished by his bequest of $1 million in land and money what he couldn't manage while alive: a successful new school of higher education—the Case School of Applied Science, on Rockwell Ave. It was the first independent school of technology west of the Alleghenies.

The Cases were doing their business friends a favor because industry had become complicated; special skills were needed, and the idea was that sons of middle-class families could afford to give up working for wages while they studied for better jobs. As for the sons and daughters of Cleveland's elite, they would continue to be taught liberal arts at tiny Western Reserve University in Hudson, Ohio.

But that school was practically broke, and so the trustees were perhaps more than willing to be lured away to University Circle

A portion of Amasa Stone's railroad fortune
helped build Western Reserve University.
(Western Reserve Historical Society)

in Cleveland by that man whose personality was as flinty as his name—Amasa Stone.

Stone's arrogance had made him unpopular even in his own top-drawer society circle. But it also drove him as a philanthropist to do things for which only he would get the credit—and that included competing with the Cases by bankrolling a successful university in Cleveland.

Stone had made a phenomenal climb to wealth and power since those early railroad days. From banking to contracting, from a rolling mill to screw manufacturing, even to a trotting track in Glenville, Amasa Stone was in the thick of it. He gave the Home for the Aged Protestant Gentlewomen to the YWCA, saw his two daughters married extremely well—Clara to John Hay, a famous diplomat, writer and secretary to Abraham Lincoln; and Flora to industrialist Samuel Mather.

But tragedy dogged him: his son, Adelbert, was drowned in a swimming accident at Yale. He lost his reputation when a train on one of his own lines plunged into the Ashtabula gorge during a snowstorm in December 1876, killing 92 passengers and injuring more. The main arch of the bridge had caved in—a wooden bridge, designed, patented, and built by Stone himself, against the advice of his own engineer who wanted a new stone or iron bridge to span the gorge.

His physical and psychological health was already bad by 1880, when his business empire began to collapse; only philanthropy relieved some of the pressure.

Stone offered the little Hudson college $500,000 if it would move to what is now the University Circle area. There were conditions: he wanted the school named for himself, (but had to settle for Adelbert College of Western Reserve University); wanted to design and construct the buildings; Cleveland citizens had to provide the land for the site; and the site had to be built next to the new Case School, which had bought some farmland east of Euclid Ave. and E. 107th St.

Leonard Case Jr. may have been dead, but Amasa Stone was still competing with the family name. The little Hudson school lunged at the offer. As a local writer put it, according to historian William G. Rose, they "hitched their educational wagon to the new star of progress and threw old-fashioned prudence to the wind."

A depressed Amasa Stone commited suicide in 1883, but his youngest daughter Flora and her husband, Samuel Mather, would help more than 30 religious, charitable and educational institutions in their time, including establishing the women's undergraduate school at Western Reserve.

And Florence and sister Clara were able to honor their autocratic father with the Amasa Stone Chapel.

There was one thing he wanted that he didn't get: a demand that the two schools exist side-by-side "in close proximity and harmony." The two institutions promptly built a fence between them.

The Sporting Life: How Golf, Football Started in Cleveland

The origins of Clevelanders' fascination with golf are linked to the wealthy magnates of the late 19th century, but the city's football mania began on a much more democratic note.

Golf was Samuel Mather's game. He had taken his distinguished old Puritan name, and his inherited fortune and made it even larger with iron ore, coal and lake shipping interests. Also, he was a master shipbuilder of lake steamers. He was a dedicated, thoughtful philanthropist, backing hospitals and educational institutions. But when he socialized he wanted to be with his friends, so, when he brought golf to Cleveland in 1895, he did it his way.

In those days, golf was a game for lady and gentleman amateurs. The pros—those grubby people who played the game for money—weren't socially acceptable. The New York Times wrap-up of the 1895 golf season didn't even mention the U.S. Open winner. But the U.S. Amateur championship, played two days before on the same course, got tremendous press coverage. The amateur players used some of the pros as their caddies—the same ones who would compete in the Open.

John D. Rockefeller had his own private course at his Forest Hills estate where he had two boys working for him, each earning 12 cents per hour (2 cents over his going rate). One would hold an umbrella over his head while the other pedaled him on his bike from hole to hole.

Mather got hooked on the game at the famous St. Andrews Club in Yonkers, N.Y., and came home and organized the Cleveland Golf Club in Glenville.

Cleveland at that time was the seventh largest city in the country with 380,000 population, but Glenville was still a beautiful, secluded rural village where top-drawer Cleveland society kept summer homes. When the Cleveland Golf Club opened July 13, 1885, The Plain Dealer didn't report it on the sports pages: "A practice game of golf at the Country Club in Glenville was quite a

Golf was one of John D. Rockefeller's (right) favorite pastimes. *(CSU)*

society event," said the newspaper. "About 50 ladies and gentlemen were present and watched the game, after which they partook of tea served by Mrs. Samuel Mather." The key words were, "quite a society event." It would be many years before the game spread to other Clevelanders.

Cleveland football began in the 1880s when anybody could play. There were no goal posts, and participants wore old clothes and made up the rules as they went along. The game featured a flying wedge—a mass of players with the ball-holder protected behind a V-formation that churned its way forward against tacklers, leaving bodies strewn in its wake.

It took brute strength to advance the ball, and no one, even in the mid-'80s, wore pads and helmets. (The forward pass didn't become legal until 1906 and wasn't really understood until Notre Dame quarterback Gus Dorais passed to end Knute Rockne and beat favored Army in 1913.)

Local interest in the game began to grow when Ivy League

school grads returned to Cleveland with stories about this wild game. College football came to the city in 1887 when the Case School of Applied Science freshmen played mighty Central High School—and got wiped out 12-0.

It wasn't until the fall of 1890 that Central High played the newly founded University School on its field at Hough & Giddings, and this time Central took a 26-0 beating from the sons of Cleveland's wealthiest industrialists. The Central boys wore any clothes they could scrape together, but the University preppies, hair neatly parted in the middle, had helmets, matching jerseys, vests, padded pants and shin guards. Both schools continued to play local college teams until football became more formalized after the turn of the century.

In December 1891, 400 fans paid 25 cents each to see the Case School "Scientists" beat the Adelbert Academy of Western Reserve College at YMCA Park (near Cedar Avenue). Three days later, the same teams played in Hudson at the Adelbert field, and the Scientists whipped them again, using a potent new weapon for the first time—the field goal.

By this time, college administrators began to realize that they could make money with this crowd-pleasing game.

Big-time football was on its way, to the country and to Cleveland's "Dawg Pound."

Churches Bore Load of Charity, Schooling

Schooling, charity and churches went hand-in-hand in early Cleveland.

A church mission group founded a school down in the Flats in the 1830s for the children of their poorest parishioners—so poor, that the school became known as "The Ragged School"; the city eventually took over its financing, renaming it the Industrial School, with the stated goal of changing "scholars from dangerous to industrious citizens."

Churches spent their charity money strictly on their own parishioners. As the City Mission of the Euclid Street Presbyterian Church bluntly put it, "No continued or permanent relief would be granted any family not connected with some Protestant congregation." These Protestant churches, (there were 34 by 1860) got together to take care of their own homeless kids with the formation of the Protestant Orphan Asylum, and that same year there were separate Catholic churches supporting their orphan asylums and schools for their mostly Irish and German congregations.

In 1873 Bishop Richard Gilmour threatened to deny the sacrament to parents of public school children. The city's small German-Jewish population took care of their own, establishing the Jewish Orphan Asylum in 1868, which would eventually become Bellefaire.

By the 1880s, there were dozens of orphanages, soup kitchens, and homes for the aged, operated mostly by religious denominations. They joined forces to coordinate fund-raising, but it wasn't enough—they were being swamped by unemployed people. Financial depressions were becoming more severe; thousands of penniless immigrants continued to pour into ethnic neighborhoods like the old Haymarket District, southwest of Public Square on lower Central Ave. and Ontario St.—"Baghdad on the Cuyahoga," it was called.

European newcomers crowded into boardinghouses and tar-papered shacks with no water or sanitation facilities; one bathtub

John D. Rockefeller helped fund Alta House, which provided a community center, classes and a nursery to Little Italy. *(CSU)*

per 600 people, a survey found. A reporter wrote of half-naked children lying in the alleys or seeking shelter under a wagon or car, as well as people sleeping on roofs to escape the summer heat. One account read: "Any Clevelander can appreciate his home 20-fold if he will but spend a few hours in going through this congested district. . . . We see here the ideal sweatshop, the father and mother 'sewing on' cheap garments at poor pay, with possibly one or more children ill in bed in the same room, and the whole surrounded by dirt and filth.'

By the 1890s, Cleveland's upper-middle-class women started to take charity leadership away from the churches. The new social gospel stressed that the roots of poverty lay in social and economic inequality, not in a lack of moral fiber. Men and women started settlement houses to care for alcoholics, single mothers and the elderly, making the city one of the country's leaders in the movement.

But prejudices die hard. When George Bellamy, together with fellow Hiram College religious students, established Hiram House on Orange Ave. to serve poor, Jewish immigrants living in the Central-Woodland neighborhood, church officials turned down his requests for help. Historian John Grabowski quotes one: "You ought to be ostracized for living among such people. God never intended to save such people. You should shove them off in a corner and let them rot."

Philanthropists like Samuel and Flora Stone Mather came to the rescue. Later, allied with the Old Stone Church, they established the famous Goodrich House. John D. Rockefeller helped finance Alta House in Murray Hill's Little Italy. It had a dispensary, public baths, a laundry and a playground.

Goodrich House, E. 6th St. and St. Clair Ave., would keep moving east with each successive wave of newcomers—Irish, Germans, Eastern Europeans, whites from Appalachia, blacks from the South.

By the 1920s, Cleveland had about a dozen settlement houses, some of them nationally famous like Karamu House for black theater, or the Cleveland Music School Settlement, pioneer in the use of music therapy.

Cleveland's social consciousness was changing and expanding as the city's ethnic balance changed, but the handful of industrialists were tired of being beseiged for donations. In 1919, they would form the Cleveland Community Fund (United Way Services), the organization that raised money for 88 organizations, mostly from employee contributions, with highly organized fund-raising drives.

Some people rejected this kind of charity. Dr. Louis Tuckerman, a clergyman, said, "Your society, with its board of trustees made up of steel magnates, coal operators and employers, is not really interested in charity. If it were, it would stop the 12-hour day; it would increase wages and put an end to the cruel killing and maiming of men."

But organized, efficient, bureaucratic fund-raising was here to stay. Foundations and charities, here and across the country, have adopted the ideas that inspired the founders of the "Ragged School" many years ago: that the community has a responsibility to help those who can't help themselves.

Big-Wheel Bikes Introduced Cleveland to Sport It Loved

Club and Races Took Off Early

Mountain bikes, helmets, tight pants and high socks are all the latest craze in exercise. But biking has been around Cleveland more than 100 years.

According to historian William G. Rose, biking was introduced to the city by two vaudevillians, the Hanlon Brothers, in 1869, when they used a clumsy, iron-tired "Rube Goldberg" contraption in their popular shows. Then, one summer day in the early 1880s, Jeptha Wade Jr., son of the Western Union telegraph tycoon, astonished the locals by heading down Euclid Ave. towards the Square perched on top of a bike with a huge front wheel—58 inches to be exact— and a tiny rear wheel, both with solid rubber tires.

Wade, with his handlebar mustache and jockey cap, apparently looked frightened way up there on his saddle since there was no easy way to get up or down. These bikes, called "ordinaries," sold very well in Cleveland.

Then the modern version, the "safety" bike, came out in the mid-1880s with two, equal-sized wheels, and this caught on quickly with office workers, schoolchildren, women and racing enthusiasts. Reports speak of Public Square being jammed with bicycles, pedestrians and carriages.

Dress designers got smart and cut out the wide skirts and bustles in favor of practical dresses that wouldn't get entangled in a bicycle's chain drive. (The same dresses also worked for that great new game everybody was playing in front of their Euclid Ave. homes, lawn tennis.)

Pneumatic tires and the air pump were introduced in the 1890s, as was the "social wheel," a tandem bike, the "bicycle-built-for-two" of song and romance.

Bicycle clubs were organized, and racing at Athletic Park's quarter-mile cinder track at Payne and Oliver streets became the sports

Bike clubs began in the Cleveland area as early as the late 1800s. *(CSU)*

rage. Competitors came from all over the Midwest and East to compete against the Cleveland Athletic Club, and the biggest one, the Cleveland Wheel Club.

The latter held the first national race in the city one hot August day in 1892, with 2,000 fans jamming the park. The night before the race, the bikers decorated their racers and tandems with lanterns and rode slowly through the night in a parade from Public Square to Athletic Field and back again.

Women bikers held a six-day race at Central Armory several years later that drew tremendous crowds, and a Forest City Ramblers club member rode 6,666 miles in nine months.

Local manufacturers like Alexander Winton and the White Sewing Machine Co. got into the picture with the latter company making 10,000 bikes per year by the mid-'90s. (These same local companies, Winton and White, would prove to be part of the undoing of mass bicycling when they began churning out the latest high-tech marvel, the horseless carriage.)

News of national bicycle races filled the sports pages of the six local newspapers and were given equal prominence with the Cleveland Spiders baseball team. There were 50,000 bikes in the city by that time.

A July, 1895, Plain Dealer carries an ad on the sports page for a $100 bicycle, "The Excelsior Light Roadster," which J.L. Hudson, their "Sole Agents," will now sell for $49. The ad goes on, "Over 500 now in use in Cleveland vicinity. A strictly high-grade 1895 Wheel, fully guaranteeed for one year. Repairs can be had through us at any time . . . Then, "names furnished of people who are riding it— ask them how they like it. . . . "

Then there was the news of the national bicycle races being held at Asbury Park, N.J., which had some Clevelanders competing in front of 9,000 spectators: " . . . a fearful storm broke out, streaks of forked lightning darted hither and thither among the clouds . . . pieces of frozen rain fell on the roofs of the grandstand that were as large as campaign buttons . . . the track was totally flooded.

City's Centennial Brought Much to Celebrate

Development, Jobs Marks of Prosperity

Clevelanders were in the mood for self-congratulations, for optimistic looking-ahead during their centennial celebration on July 22, 1896.

There didn't seem to be any room for doubts on that day as the cannon from the Ohio Light Artillery boomed and church bells chimed from Trinity Cathedral on the Square.

And why should there have been any doubts? When a town goes from a wilderness clearing in the middle of nowhere to a booming city of over 261,000,—the 10th biggest in the United States—you do have something to crow about. From the grimy, smoky Cuyahoga Valley where more than 30 foreign tongues were spoken, to the lofty-tree-lined suburbs where the older, white, native-born stock had congregated, there was agreement on one thing: The city had jobs, and jobs meant prosperity. Never mind that the railroads had destroyed the beauty of the lakefront, cutting down the elms, hickory and oak to make way for their tracks; never mind that railroad and factory smoke was choking those immigrants jammed into the Valley's homes—the payrolls they created were the important things.

The Early Settler's Association had built a huge log cabin in Public Square where they posed for photographs, aging children and grandchildren of the original New Englanders. A huge arch, patterned after the Arc de Triomphe in Paris, straddled Superior Ave. and was ringed with hundreds of the new electric arc lights that Cleveland's own Charles Brush had invented. The crowd gasped when President Grover Cleveland, a distant relative of Moses Cleaveland, pushed a button back in Buzzard's Bay, Mass., and the lights on the arch magically lit up.

Cleveland's downtown skyline looked different, too—new high-rise office buildings poked up, as high as 14 stories! The famous

Public Square during the Cleveland Centennial Celebration in 1896. *(CSU)*

Arcade had already hosted the National Republican League's banquet the year before—a tribute to the political power of Mark Hanna. Inter-urban electric trolleys were delivering passengers from 11 lines into Public Square from all over northeast Ohio, and would soon run to Detroit and Erie.

Cleveland companies were the biggest shipbuilders in the United States. They controlled most of the mines and ore on the Great Lakes, led the world in production of Bessemer steel, pig iron and steel rails, made huge quantities of chemicals, refined oil products, textiles, sewing machines, bicycles, electric-light carbons. You name it, it was made here—maybe had been invented here, like chewing gum.

The Cleveland Public library pioneered open-shelf libraries and branch libraries, opening up self-education and enjoyment to thousands of children and adults who had never had a book in their homes, never before had the pleasure of browsing through library aisles to their hearts' content.

Then, too, Cleveland's social consciousness was awakening.

George Bellamy had opened the Hiram House, the first settlement house in Ohio in the middle of the Whiskey Island's Irish on the near West Side. He was just barely keeping it alive out of his own pocket and some rural church funds, but the Mathers would soon come to the rescue.

Some 50,000 men and women bikers were running around the streets, going to work and school, racing and just generally enjoying themselves.

The Cleveland Spiders baseball team, with the legendary battery of Cy Young and "Chief" Zimmer, had won the National League's Temple Cup (the World Series of that day) the year before from—you guessed it—the Baltimore Orioles. They would lose it that year to the same team, playing before crowds in both towns that were so rowdy that the word "fans," derived from "fanatics," was first used to describe them, according to historian John Grabowski.

John Ellesler's Euclid Street Opera House staged George Bernard Shaw's plays with actors and actresses whose names still ring a bell: Sarah Bernhardt, Ethel Barrymore, Richard Mansfield.

But all wasn't fun and games in centennial Cleveland. There were thousands of desperately poor people living hard and bitter lives who would have cursed the name, "Gay Nineties"! Perhaps acknowledging this, the Women's Department of the Centennial Commission deposited a time capsule that said, in part:

"We bequeath to you a city of a century, prosperous and beautiful, and yet far from our ideal. . . . Many of the people are poor. And some are vainly seeking work at living wages. Sometimes some of the reins of government slip from the hands of the people, and public honors ill fit some who wear them. . . .

"Some of our children are robbed of their childhood. Vice parades our streets, and disease lurks in many places. We are obliged to confess that even now, man's inhumanity to man makes countless thousands mourn. How are these things with you? . . . Have you invented a flying machine or found the North Pole? What have you done? . . . "

Well . . . "Yes," to the flying machine and the North Pole.

Tom Johnson Rode Streetcars into Mayor's Office

It has been said the social conscience of Cleveland has never been at ease since Tom L. Johnson's days as a reform mayor of Cleveland.

When he became mayor in 1901, the office was a place where political buddies would stop in for drinks and cigars. Nobody in Cleveland, or for that matter anywhere else, was thinking of using the mayor's office for social activism.

Lincoln Steffens, the famous muckraking journalist, was beginning to talk about "the shame of the cities," and the system of "bosses and boodle," but Cleveland wasn't listening until Tom Loftin Johnson became mayor.

Johnson took an unlikely route to the mayor's office and international fame as a radical populist reformer. He was a self made multimillionaire, and could have been expected to have been a bulwark of the Republican Party. But he was a red-hot Democrat who blasted bloated wealth and privilege in both parties.

Johnson was born in a small town in Kentucky, the son of a real Confederate Kentucky colonel who lost everything in the Civil War. The family ended up near Louisville where 15-year-old Tom got a job with a small street railway company as a clerk at $7 a week. Two years later, he was general superintendent of the line.

He invented a coin fare box, sold it to his own and other railways for a $30,000 profit. This money, and all he could borrow, was put up to buy a losing Indianapolis traction company that he turned into a profitable operation. Then Johnson began to look around for bigger game and found it in the Cleveland railway jungle, with eight street railway lines and a fierce, dominating lion named Mark Hanna.

That didn't bother the young tiger; when he arrived in Cleveland in 1879 at the age of 25, he had a plan. The city was booming with a population of more than 160,000, and more immigrants were arriving daily; they needed cheap transportation to factory, office and home, and in 1880, that meant horse-drawn streetcars.

None of Hanna's routes interconnected; a passenger had to pay a new fare each time he got on a different line. Hanna also owned a little one-half-mile line that was the vital link connecting East and West sides at the Superior St. Viaduct. Johnson bought a small West Side railway company that ran right up to that line, he was turned down cold when he requested permission to interconnect with it.

To get his cars over the viaduct to downtown Cleveland, he had to haul his passengers in horse-drawn buses. But to the shock of all Cleveland, when it came time for City Council to consider renewing the franchise for Hanna's line, Johnson raised such a political storm by attacking monopolies and "privilege" that council wouldn't grant the renewal unless Hanna's line let Johnson's cars use its tracks

Then, according to Cleveland historian George Condon, Johnson moved quickly to capitalize on his new civic and political stature by buying a second railway line and bidding in City Council for a franchise to build East Side railway lines; the idea was to connect his West Side holdings with these to provide Cleveland's first cross-city transportation for a single low fare. After Johnson and Hanna battled at every public council meeting, several councilmen considered to be in Hanna's "pocket" switched their votes to Johnson and gave him an astounding victory.

Mark Hanna was puzzled; he and Johnson were both successful big businessmen who had made a lot of money from monopolies. What were they fighting about? Why couldn't they work together instead of against each other? So Hanna invited Johnson to lunch at the Union Club and proposed a partnership, which Johnson promptly turned down.

As Tom Johnson explained in his autobiography later, "We were too much alike; as associates it would be a question . . . of a short time only until one of us would 'crowd the other clear off the bench'; that we would make good opponents but poor partners.' And, said Johnson, "I have never had any occasion to modify that opinion."

But being a tough, successful businessman isn't what earned Tom Johnson his statue on Public Square. That honor would come about through politics—for a man who had never even voted.

Hanna Was at the Forefront of U.S., City Politics

You can't talk about the political history of the United States or Cleveland in the late 19th century without taking Mark Hanna's career and times into account.

He was more than just Tom Johnson's chief antagonist during the early years of the street railway wars. He was the Boss of Bosses of the Republican Party, the man who could make a president, tough, brilliant and ruthless.

And Mark Hanna was nobody's hired puppet; he firmly believed that if Big Business was left alone to make big profits, it would employ more workers, pay them better wages, and they in turn would buy more American goods, keeping the wheels turning in a beautiful circle. Later generations would call this the "trickle-down theory."

Hanna was born to prosperous New Lisbon, Ohio, parents, Dr. Leonard and Samantha Hanna, who moved to Cleveland in 1852 when the Ohio Canal bypassed their town. Mark was 16 years old when he attended Central High School, where his classmates in- cluded the Rockefeller brothers, William and John D., and the lat- ter's future bride, Laura Spelman.

Young Hanna enrolled at Western Reserve College in Hudson in 1857, and departed after only four months to his and the college's mutual relief; apparently, the college didn't appreciate his practical jokes.

Mark got a job in his family's wholesale grocery and commis- sion house business in the Flats, where he kept the books, acted as purser on their lake steamers, and was a traveling salesman through Indiana, Ohio, and Illinois.

Mark Hanna cast his first Republican vote in 1860 for Abraham Lincoln, and wanted to enlist a year later when the Civil War broke out. But he was the only one who knew the family business inside out; he stayed, and brother Howard joined the army.

Mark met Charlotte Augusta Rhodes of Franklin Circle at a

Mark Hanna built a power base in Cleveland industry but
is best remembered for his hard work and zeal for the
Republican Party. *(Cleveland Public Library)*

bazaar about a year later, and she returned his affections. But she
was the daughter of Dan Rhodes, the richest coal-and-iron merchant in town and the town's leading Democrat, and he didn't want
his daughter to marry any "damned black Republican." True love
and Cleveland society, who wanted this match, persevered; Mark
and Charlotte were married at St. John's Episcopal church in September 1864.

Now Hanna set to work building a business empire: lake steamers, iron ore, his father-in-law's coal mines, oil refining—and Cleveland politics. But here he found that he couldn't interest his friends
in, say, a Republican caucus, and he bored them by pushing them
to attend political meetings or give up their duck-hunting and go to
the polls on Election Day. Years later, he would say, "Your newspapers used to gas about the great excitement of some election . . . and
then we had to hire livery hacks to get the voters to come and vote!"

Local Republican machine politics infuriated him with their
buying and selling of immigrant votes, so much so, in fact, that he

and some fellow Republicans bolted the party in 1873 to help elect a reputable Democratic mayor.

That was the year that the worst financial panic in America's history—up to that point—broke out. Hundreds of thousands were thrown out of work as banks and stock markets collapsed, and businesses, mines and railroads failed. The price of coal, along with everything else, plummeted. When mine owners cut wages, a new coal miners union was organized and sent delegates to beg the owners for living wages. Only Mark Hanna even listened to them, and offered to help them. He had formed a coal operators association and believed in what would now be called collective bargaining. Hanna also believed, his son said in later years, "that some corporations and large industrial concerns were deliberately bleeding their workmen as a matter of selfish economy."

When operators reduced wages again in 1876—against Hanna's advice—the union couldn't keep the men from striking. Two of Hanna's mines were set on fire, the militia was called out, and a company employee shot. Hanna found himself, as head of the operators association, with the responsibility of seeing that 23 half-starved miners were punished by law.

No reputable lawyer from the mine counties would touch the case except one: Major William McKinley of Canton, a staunch Republican who was being mentioned as a congressional candidate. McKinley would win his clients' freedom—and he would win something much more that would change his life forever: the respect and admiration of his courtroom opponent, Marcus Alonzo Hanna.

Tom Johnson, Hero for Common Citizen

Cleveland business tycoon Tom Johnson was a badly shaken man in 1883. He had read economist Henry George's book, "Social Problems," and correctly interpreted it as a condemnation of everything he had stood for as a freewheeling capitalist entrepreneur.

The money he had made by investing in street railways in Cleveland and eight other cities and the steel mills he owned were seen by George as wealth gathered through the use of monopolies that had resulted in increasing poverty for others; or, as the famous social reformer called it, "privilege."

Henry George saw land as being a free gift of nature, and since he saw private property as the source of the problem, advocated common ownership of all land, and he wanted every tax abolished except a single tax on land.

Johnson squirmed. Was he a part of the problem? At a time when powerful industrial barons liked to crush labor unions, Johnson ran shops with liberal wages, reasonable hours and safe working conditions. And he didn't honor blacklists.

In a visit to George in Brooklyn in 1885 Johnson said he would have to get out of business if the book was right. Henry George convinced Johnson to stay put. "Make all the money you can, even if you do not believe in the methods of getting riches; for in your case, these same riches, taken from the people by the laws giving special privileges, will be used for the common good, in overthrowing these same laws."

So Tom Johnson stayed in business, studying politics and learning public speaking. Then he ran for the Democratic congressional seat in Cleveland's 21st District in 1888. He lost but was elected in 1890 in what would turn out to be two terms fighting big business, at some cost to his own interests.

But Johnson was interested in Cleveland, and the leaders of the Democratic Party in the city were ready for him—particularly his money. They were fed up with their own party's mayor, John Farley,

Mayor Thomas Johnson could often be seen riding in a Winton "Red Devil."
(Cleveland Public Library)

who was influenced by conservative financial backing. Johnson was a smart choice. Not only did workingmen back him, but even some businessmen saw him as one of their own: "A chance to get good government and a $100,000-a-year man for mayor for $6,000," one of them said.

Owners of steam railroads knew what was coming: They rushed an ordinance through City Council giving them $20 million of lakefront land without paying a cent. Johnson, operating as a citizen, obtained an injunction to stop the giveaway, but the injunction was to expire April 4. Johnson was elected mayor April 1, 1901. The Board of Elections had to be pushed night and day to certify him as mayor in three days. When he took the oath of office the morning of the 4th, he had 37 minutes before the injunction expired. Johnson went to the mayor's office, and in his words: "Mr. Farley looked up as I came in, and mumbled, 'Well, Tom, when are you going to take hold?' I replied that I hoped he would take his time about moving his belongings, but that I had been mayor for several minutes." In a few minutes, Johnson ended the "Great Railroad Giveaway."

It was only the start. Johnson was 47 when he became mayor in what would be the first of four terms, a blunt-talking, 260-pound dynamo who involved himself in everything from tax reform to garbage collection. He picked his cabinet on the basis of ability, not political loyalty.

With the increase in crime on everybody's mind, he appointed an arrogant, tough police captain, Fred Kohler, a Republican, to be his new chief to clean up a corrupt police force that had let gambling and prostitution run wild.

Newton Baker, a brilliant young lawyer, would be his legal ace. Johnson would write in his autobiography, "Mr. Baker was really head of the cabinet and principal adviser to us all. . . . He ranks with the best, highest-paid corporation lawyers in ability and has held his public office at a constant personal sacrifice. This low-paid official has seen every day in the courtroom lawyers getting often five times the fee for bringing a suit than he got for defending it. He did for the people for love what other lawyers did for corporations for money."

Then there was Dr. Harris Cooley, his own minister, appointed director of the Department of Charities and Corrections, marking a new era in social-service work, according to historian Eugene Murdock. "What I want for this position is a man of judgment and heart," said Johnson, ". . . I want him in my cabinet to look after the workhouse inmates, where men and women are often treated like dogs, and to protect the city's poor and infirm, so badly provided for."

Now Tom Johnson was ready to tilt his lance against Privilege—and make Cleveland world-famous for its progressive politics!

Johnson's Peak Years Were
Rife with Politics

Cleveland newspapers of 1903 would have an oddly familiar ring to anybody reading them today. Mayor Tom Johnson was fighting monopoly, as he had promised, and his target was the Cleveland Electric Illuminating Co., which he felt was overcharging the city.

Johnson battled futilely to get a bond issue passed to build a city plant; when that failed, he went after a small lighting plant that the independent community of South Brooklyn had just built. His idea was to annex the community, an idea that Brooklyn's mayor and most of its citizens heartily approved of because they wanted access to Cleveland's cheaper water and better school system.

When both Cleveland and South Brooklyn balloted 8 to 1 in favor of annexation it looked like a done deal, but it was only the beginning of a real donnybrook between Tom Johnson and CEI. It was two years later, in 1905, before Cleveland got its hands on the little municipal lighting plant. As for CEI, it began an annual reduction of the prices it charged city users.

Tom Johnson still had to fight the artificial-gas companies. The East Ohio Gas Co., (natural gas) was a subsidiary of John D. Rockefeller's Standard Oil Co., the original and most powerful trust in the world. So when East Ohio officials appeared before City Council for a franchise to pump natural gas from their West Virginia fields up to Cleveland, everybody knew what Tom Johnson's answer would be. Everybody was wrong!

The mayor told East Ohio that if it would supply cheaper gas to the city and not try to finagle ("boodle") with City Council, he would support it. Since the powerful coal companies supplied the artificial-gas companies, and there were millions of dollars involved in the franchise award, there apparently was "boodling" to spare. But the good guys won again, and the natural-gas ordinance was approved.

The mayor and Dr. Harris Cooley, director of the Department of Charities and Corrections, made frequent visits to the city work-

Thomas L. Johnson created many progressive social programs in the early 20th century. *(Cleveland Public Library)*

house, and began pardoning applicants on a scale never seen in Cleveland before. After one year in office, the two men freed 463 inmates—52 would be jailed again.

The police and the newspaper, the Leader, began attacking Cooley for turning criminals out on the streets and creating a "crime wave." Cooley defended himself ably, but in response to the criticisms, hired one of the first regular parole officers in the country, and founded a night school at the workhouse—another first.

And then came the famous Farm Colonies, which gained national and international attention. The idea was to have criminals, the sick, the insane and the elderly live in a healthy, country atmosphere. The city bought 2,200 acres in Warrensville Heights, where it built a new workhouse, poorhouse and TB sanitarium.

The corrections facility was run on the unheard-of honor system—no guards, no prison clothes, no barbed-wire fences.

Now the national newspapers began to pay attention to Cleveland's reform mayor; the Ohio state Democratic Party finally woke up, and in 1903 nominated Johnson for governor. This aroused the old "boss of bosses," Republican Sen. Mark Hanna. Tom Johnson was his old enemy from the street-railway wars, and even more infuriating, had won two terms as mayor against the opposition of the most powerful politician in the country, the man who had put President McKinley in office—and a Clevelander. So Hanna made deals with conservative Democrats all over the state who were as bitterly opposed to Johnsonian reform measures as the Republicans were.

Cleveland's leading banker, Myron Herrick, was Johnson's opponent, and he and Hanna came out swinging. Herrick said, "We all believe in home rule . . . But the real issue of the campaign is the attempt being made to foist the single tax, and socialism, on the state." Hanna chimed in with, ". . . I charge that Tom L. Johnson is the national leader of the Socialist party. Under the guise of the cloak of democracy he is striving to accomplish results . . . to meet his own selfish ends. I beg of you to rise and kill the attempt to float the flag of socialism over Ohio."

The big fellow never had a chance and was swamped by rural votes in one of the worst defeats in Democratic state history.

And so Tom Johnson came back to Cleveland—with his greatest years still ahead of him.

Boss Hanna Was Cartoonists' Favorite Target

Teddy Roosevelt once said of Mark Hanna that, "The oddest thing about Hanna was that numbers of intelligent people thought him a fool . . . "

Well, Mark Hanna WAS a very complex man who became to political cartoonists the embodiment of the bloated, corrupt, political boss, representing the rich against the worker.

The Hearst papers characterized him as the Red Boss of Cleveland politics, ruling the city from his office, terrorizing unions and ruining rival street railways . . . "He sent poor sailors out to sea on his ships on the wintry Lakes, cold and starving, unpaid and mutinous. He had corrupted Gov. William McKinley's government, etc."

And yet, according to his biographer, Thomas Beer, when fellow Republican George Pullman brought on a very violent general strike in 1894 by his refusal to negotiate with his workers, Hanna raged against him publicly in the Union Club: "The damned idiot ought to arbitrate! What did he think he was doing? A man who won't meet his men halfway is a [expletive] fool." And this was the same man who lent his money to Union veterans so they could attend Ulysses Grant's funeral in New York.

In 1894, Mark Hanna, president of a bank, director of street railways, partner in three rolling mills, executive in a ship-building company, gave up all these businesses to devote himself full time to getting his friend, Ohio's Gov. William McKinley, elected president of the United States.

By the time the Republican convention gathered in 1896, Mark Hanna's organizing ability and drive, and $100,000 spent out of his own pocket, had already sewn up a majority of the delegates for his candidate. Then came the amazing, so-called "Front Porch" presidential campaign. McKinley didn't want to campaign away from his invalid wife, and he couldn't match Democratic candidate William Jennings Bryan's oratory, so Hanna moved the campaign to his front porch in Canton. The governor made dozens of speeches a day to large crowds brough in by the railroads at discount rates.

According to Cleveland historian George Condon, Hanna flooded the country with 30 million pieces of McKinley literature a week, had his face on drinking mugs, posters, badges, spoons and lapel buttons. Little boys sang: "McKinley drinks soda water, Bryan drinks rum; McKinley is a gentleman, Bryan is a bum!"

Successful? McKinley won the 1896 election by more than 600,000 votes.

The new president, and his "political prime minister," as one observer called Hanna, upset the accepted wisdom when the president appointed political moderates to his Cabinet, and paid very little attention to Wall Street. Everybody figured Hanna wanted to be secretary of the Treasury, but he said to a friend, "Me in the Cabinet? All the newspapers would have cartoons of me stealing the White House kitchen stove!"

What he did want was to be U.S. senator from Ohio so he could help his great friend McKinley be a successful president. This was neatly arranged by the appointment of Ohio's Sen. John Sherman as secretary of state, and having the Republican governor of Ohio appoint Hanna to succeed him for the remaining year of his term.

But that year was soon up, and Hanna at the age of 60—a man who had never faced a voter—was going to have to face election before the Ohio Assembly—that's the way it was done then.

The campaign turned out to be just possibly the meanest, nastiest, most bitterly fought senatorial election in American history. Biographer Herbert Croly, says, "He [Hanna] was portrayed as a monster of sordid greed, as the embodiment of all that was worst in American politics and business."

Hanna campaigned across the state, speaking in large cities and small towns; audiences liked his blunt, plain-spoken ways.

In January of 1898, with the state Assembly ready to vote, this is how Croly saw it: "Columbus came to resemble a medieval city given over to an angry feud between armed partisans. Blows were exchanged in hotels and on the streets. There were threats of assassination. Timid men feared to go out after dark . . . " The 73 legislators who were committed to Mark Hanna were marched under armed guard to the Statehouse to vote for their man and give him a three-vote margin of victory!

Mark Hanna's star would never shine brighter!

Rockefeller, the Mastermind of Monopoly

Long before anyone ever dreamed of finding oil in Oklahoma or Texas, Cleveland's John D. Rockefeller had made himself the richest man in the world from western Pennsylvania oil.

Refining oil was John D.'s game; not wildcatting for it. That was too dangerous and unpredictable for the man who worshiped control.

Young Rockefeller had first visited the shantytowns of the Pennsylvania oilfields in 1860, found "chaos and disorder, waste and incompetence, competition at its worst." The dislike was mutual; oil-field roughnecks called the 21-year-old "that bloodless Baptist bookkeeper." Their dislike would deepen to hatred in a few years when he began to get control of the oil-refining business and provided the producers with their worst fear: a monopoly buyer.

By 1863, in the middle of the Civil War, Rockefeller and his partner, Maurice Clark, with two of Clark's brothers, opened their Excelsior works refinery on 3 acres at Kingsbury Run where it met the Cuyahoga River. There were trees still standing there from before Moses Cleaveland's arrival. It was one of 20 new refineries along the river distilling western Pennsylvania crude into the great new lighting fuel that everyone wanted: kerosene.

A railroad linked Cleveland with the oilfields and shipped the distilled products to the Eastern seaboard. The once clear and sparkling Cuyahoga was now covered with a viscous scum, the smoky skies were spoiling the butter in the spring houses and the beer in the breweries in the Flats; fire engines clanged through the streets putting out fires from that unwanted distilling byproduct, gasoline.

Rockefeller later clashed with the Clark brothers over policy, auctioned off the firm's assets, and then outbid the brothers for them, keeping only the man he wanted, Samuel Andrews, his chemist.

As Rockefeller saw it, his mission was to drive his competitors out of business so he could keep his profit margins high. The way to do this was to reduce his production costs, make his Standard

(Top) John D. Rockefeller located his first refinery on
this hillside in 1863. In this photo, taken about 1870,
cows can be seen grazing in the foreground. (Bottom)
Standard Oil's operations grew dramatically in the early
20th century. *(CSU)*

Oil Co. the most efficient, best-quality refinery in the country, and
undersell his competition.

Since an important part of his costs depended on railroad freight
rates, the ruthless young entrepreneur went after the three major
railroads servicing Cleveland, and got secret rebates from them.
This worked so well that he and several other independent refiners
joined in a secret pool called the South Improvement Co. that not
only extracted secret rebates on their own rail shipments, but actually got rebates on their competitors' shipments and full information on who they were shipping to. Word leaked out and the outcry

was so loud that Standard Oil was able to buy out 21 of the other 26 Cleveland refineries.

As for Standard's suppliers, they were soon given offers they couldn't refuse: Sell out to Standard or be forced out of business. The smart ones sold out for Standard Oil stock, and became rich beyond their dreams; the ones who accepted cash lived to regret it. Sometimes they sued for more, but always became lifelong enemies of Rockefeller, including his younger brother, Frank.

John Huntington traded his asphalt roofing business for stock, went on to wealth in other fields, got into politics, gave much time and money back to the community. His Huntington Trust helped found the Cleveland Museum of Art.

As for charity, Rockefeller had tithed himself 50 cents from his first $50 paycheck and sent money that first year, at the insistence of his wife, Laura, to a Cincinnati black man "to buy his wife." Also benefiting from Rockefeller's tithing were the Ragged School and the Cleveland Bible Society, among other institutions. This giving would evolve into the Rockefeller Foundation, which poured a half-billion dollars into educational and church institutions.

In 1879, a group of independent refiners built a pipeline to the Eastern seaboard to bypass the railroads. Rockefeller built his own pipeline, cut the rates, and bought up the independents' customers. By 1879, Standard was doing 90 percent of the nation's oil refining.

A year later, with state legislatures zeroing in on him for his monopoly practices, Rockefeller formed the Standard Oil Trust to evade them—a single colossus that he controlled with a nine-member board of trustees from his empire.

Could any person or governmental unit have blocked him? Not to hear Rockefeller tell it years later: "The time was ripe for it. It had to come . . . The day of combination is here to stay. Individualism has gone, never to return."

Rockefeller's Trust Travails

John D. Rockefeller's Standard Oil Co. just kept growing and growing and growing, refining not only kerosene for lighting, its chief product, but many spinoff products such as asphalt, basic material for fertilizers, grease, oils, macadam binder, benzines and naphthas.

Standard's own wagons would deliver a can of oil to the home or corner grocery store; elephants carted it in India, donkeys and camels in North Africa; runners lit China's lamps.

But there were those pesky state charters that had to be obtained for each company. That meant state legislatures that had to be controlled. And that meant money that had to be spent to counter the rising tide of populist attacks from small businessmen and farmers.

The Rockefeller lawyers were equal to the occasion. They dreamed up the world's first trust, and, in 1882, all of the stock of the Standard Oil companies was transferred to nine trustees headed by John D. The idea was, "to exercise general supervision over the affairs of the said Stand. Oil Cos., and as far as practicable over the others Cos. or Partnerships any portion of whose stock is held in said trust."

Standard Oil of Ohio was the largest of the 14 companies included, and they in turn controlled 26 more. The Trust was capitalized at $70 million, and a quarter of its shares was owned by Rockefeller. Ida Tarbell, the famous muckraker, would write years later of the Trust: "39 [sic] corporations, each of them having legal existence, obliged by the laws of the state creating it to limit its operations to certain lines and to make certain reports, had turned over their affairs to an organization having no legal existence, independent of all authority, able to do anything it wanted anywhere; and . . . working in absolute darkness . . . you could argue its existence from its effects, but you could never prove it. You could no more grasp it than you could an eel."

The formation of the Trust successfully leapfrogged over state and local charters, creating an entity that seemed untouchable.

Rockefeller built this house at the southwest corner of E. 40th St. and Euclid Ave. in 1868, before the fights began over the trust. It was torn down in 1938. *(CSU)*

Now the Industrial Age robber barons had their role model. Now they could jump the local and state hurdles to growth and consolidation. And they did, in every field. The small retailer who tried to resist the American Tobacco Co., the small flour mill that went up against Pillsbury—they were permanently downsized.

But Tarbell's, and other journalists' attacks on trusts were having a telling effect on public opinion. Tarbell's 1904 book of her collected articles was a runaway best seller, and that year she came to Cleveland for an unannounced personal look at John D. in his lair, which turned out to be on a Sunday morning at the Euclid Avenue Baptist Church.

She had warned her readers, according to historian Grace Goulder, that he was threatening to control educational and religious institutions through his philanthropies in the same way that he had gained almost total control over petroleum refining through the ruthless use of his power.

Tarbell was impressed with that same sense of power in his

every move, but to her it was a sinister thing: "He seemed the oldest man in the world, a living mummy." His face expressed "concentration, cruelty, and craftiness;" the nose "like a thorn between puffy cheeks"; a "lipless" mouth; blank eyes; a head "swept bare of hair"; "flesh diseased and unclean." . . . there was something indescribably repulsive about him."

The Cleveland business community was outraged! Standard Oil was the biggest industry in town, had made Cleveland the international center for the petroleum refining business, and Rockefeller money was going into local education and charities.

So a group of the city's business elite called on John D. one sunny afternoon at the Rockefeller summer estate in East Cleveland, the "Homestead," and had their say about this strange, remote figure: ". . . in the creating and building up of industries . . . it is doubtful if the world ever produced a greater man than yourself. . . . There is no other record like yours in the whole world. . . . We respect you for your ability, for your integrity and your generosity in helping to build great institutions for the benefit of your fellow men. . . . We stand here to express our confidence in you and to acknowledge you as one of the great men of the age in which you live. . . . We have learned to appreciate the many gifts you have made to the city. You have taught the world how to give wisely and well."

"Indescribably repulsive?" "Great Man?"

Will the real John D. Rockefeller please stand up?

A Strong Will Gave Birth to Cleveland Orchestra

Everything was up to date in Cleveland when the Cleveland Orchestra gave its first performance at Grays Armory on Dec. 11, 1918, under the baton of Nikolai Sokoloff—exactly one month after the armistice ending World War I.

According to the local papers, you could buy a Cadillac that could make it to the West Coast in 11 days. No price was mentioned—after all, Cadillac buyers shouldn't ask. Men's madras shirts at the May Co. were $1.85, flannel shirts $5. The Winton Hotel's Rainbow Room and the Statler Hotel were advertising for New Year's Eve parties. Shubert's Colonial Theater was staging David Belasco's "The Wanderer," with a company of 125, a ballet of 50, and a flock of sheep!

But if you could afford the 25-cent admission price, the young, Russian-born conductor gave you a little shot of everything, opening with Victor Herbert, going on to Bizet, Tchaikovsky and Liadov, and closing with Liszt.

The gods and the critics were smiling on the orchestra that night. James Rogers, The Plain Dealer critic, found it "of excellent quality," and Sokoloff "a leader of capacity and resources. He hitches his chariot to a star." Wilson Smith of the Cleveland Press said delightedly, "Cleveland has at last a symphony orchestra."

It hadn't been an easy start-up. Only the determination of a very strong-willed lady, Adella Prentiss Hughes, would be able to take a grimy, brawling industrial town and turn it into a city that would someday be renowned as a music center.

Her timing was good—the conservative Euclid Ave. industrial elite were ready to pour their money back into the community. Cleveland had overtaken Cincinnati to become the largest city in Ohio, but it wasn't in the same class, culturally speaking. The Queen City had been manufacturing pianos as far back as 1820, had established a Conservatory of Music in 1867 and founded its symphony in 1895.

On November 14, 1929, John L. Severance breaks ground for the new Severance Hall. *(Cleveland Public Library)*

By contrast, the most important building in Cleveland was the Standard Oil Co.'s Refinery No. 1.

It took Hughes many years of fund-raising, of booking subscription concerts with the help of her philanthropist friends, of hiring a talented young conductor and local musicians. And then, when all was finally ready by September of 1918, everything fell apart when a killer flu struck.

"What war with all its terrors could not accomplish has yet been brought to pass," wrote The Plain Dealer. "Not Germans, but microbes have put the music-makers to flight." Schools and colleges shut their doors; public gatherings were forbidden. But the plague lifted, and so did Cleveland's spirits that December night in 1918.

Then the promotion started; Hughes and Sokoloff wanted to reach the whole family, children and businessmen. The string quartet went to public concerts and private musicales; recordings were made on the Brunswick label and broadcast on WTAM Radio. They held music memory contests for schoolchildren, pioneered in public school concerts. The orchestra was proclaimed a force for Americanization, and a women's committee was organized that went after the suburbs; the audiences grew.

Hard-sell ads were run: "If you have civic pride, patronize our Cleveland Orchestra." Popular programs were described in a 1923 ad as "pre-eminently concerts for the businessman." Another said, "Next Sunday at Masonic Hall you can hear 90 artists for the price of a ticket to a movie. Don't you want to hear a Strauss waltz, familiar opera selections, a lovely soloist, and a gorgeous orchestral piece that describes a battle? . . . All this for 50 cents?"

By the time the orchestra's brand-new Severance Hall opened its doors in February 1931, musical director Sokoloff was becoming an increasingly lonely figure up on his new podium. The maestro was caught between pleasing established conservative tastes and trying to showcase new American and European composers. And then he was a little old-fashioned with his high collars, his flamboyant, theatrical method of conducting.

One glimpse into his character: In 1930 he had contributed $100 to the cause of repealing Prohibition, whereupon Billy Sunday denounced him from the pulpit of the Euclid Ave. Baptist Church as a "dirty foreigner" for attempting to overthrow Prohibition. Sokoloff promptly doubled his contribution. But the old optimism was gone from this workingman's city, where the Depression had thrown many thousands out of work.

The plaintive tune, "Brother, Can You Spare a Dime?" said more about Cleveland's musical tastes than anything the maestro could whip up on the stage. When his contract wasn't renewed in 1932, the loyal Hughes stepped down as orchestra manager, but stayed with the Musical Arts Association, which runs the orchestra, until she died in 1950.

The man who took over the baton was Artur Rodzinski, who came to Cleveland at the peak of his career. He was 41, charming, sophisticated, and had more talent than he had the self-discipline to control. But for all the uproar the maestro created during his 10-year stay, he brought national artistic stature to the orchestra and city.

Szell Was Musical
Turning Point for City

Vienna-born Erich Leinsdorf was 31 when he replaced the dynamic Artur Rodzinski as musical director of the Cleveland Orchestra in 1943. He had been the boy wonder of the New York Metropolitan Opera when he caught the eye of Adella Prentiss Hughes, at 73 still a dominant force in Cleveland music.

The Cleveland Press stated that his appointment was a gamble "on talent, intelligence and youth rather than an established symphonic experience. . . . "

And Rodzinski was a tough act to follow. He had a loyal following and a national reputation. Board members who found Leinsdorf aloof or just plain brash were able to put off worrying about him when he was drafted into the Army in January 1944. By the time Leinsdorf was discharged and returned to Severance in the autumn of '45, his musical world had turned upside down. Orchestral standards had dropped because of the effects of the draft, and this was blamed on the conductor—not the war.

There had been a great parade of guest conductors in Cleveland during those war years, but the turning point was Nov. 2, 1944, when a conductor named George Szell walked on stage and electrified the audience with a performance the likes of which no Clevelander had ever heard before.

In December, a second series of concerts of Beethoven, French and Russian music, followed by Brahms and Bartok, swept the audience, musicians and critics completely away.

One critic said, "This was surely not the same orchestra we have been listening to all season." The Cleveland Press said, "Cleveland probably can have Mr. Szell, but on his terms and his terms only—absolute power!" Exactly. And when George Szell was made orchestra director in 1946, Cleveland's whole musical world was changed forever.

Actually, the Szell legend had been forming earlier. He was born in Budapest in 1897 of Czech background, was a child prodigy

George Szell with the Cleveland Orchestra at a concert in Prague, 1965.
(Cleveland Public Library)

who appeared in a public concert at the age of 11, and at 16 led the Vienna Philharmonic when the regular conductor fell ill. Szell was a conductor of a type that no longer exists: Philadelphia's Ormandy, Boston's Koussevitsky, NBC's Arturo Toscanini—men with a commitment to their orchestras.

Szell was a pefectionist, a taskmaster who some feared, dictatorial, as demanding in rehearsal as on the concert stage—but just as demanding of himself. Legend has it that he transformed the orchestra with one rehearsal, saying. "There are no bad orchestras, only bad conductors." True or not, he definitely did say, "where others stop playing, we begin to rehearse."

Somebody once said that "the Cleveland Orchestra plays six concerts a week and admits the public to the final two."

His repertoire emphasized the classic and romantic periods, but he did the "modern classics" also, and was hardly the Beethoven, Brahms and Schumann captive that legend would have him.

It was once said he was his own worst enemy—until the Metropolitan Opera's Rudolf Bing retorted, "Not as long as I'm alive!"

He would tell the musicians what color socks to wear, how to have their glasses adjusted, how to take a nap. He once fired a musician for driving too good a car and not spending enough on his violin. He ordered the stationery, approved record jackets, and checked the box-office receipts every morning, arriving ahead of the orchestra. He would rehearse the national anthem, "Happy Birthday," a comedy routine with Jack Benny—all with equal intensity.

Szell lived to see the realization of his dream of a summer home for his orchestra when Blossom Music Center opened in 1968, built on 500 acres in the Cuyahoga River Valley halfway between Cleveland and Akron. He died July 30, 1970, when the orchestra under Pierre Boulez was playing a concert there, leaving a city stunned.

Harold Schonberg of the New York Times said, "The world of music will miss the authoritarian, profound George Szell, he of the perfect ear and flawless technique, the master of rhythm, balances, and textures, the creator of structure in sound. . . . " Time magazine said, "He demonstrated an unswerving aural vision of how music should sound . . . and the almost psychic power of leadership to make it sound that way. . . . "

Szell would say with pride of his Cleveland Orchestra, "That is how we make music in Cleveland!" To cities all over the world, Cleveland is known today because of how the "Szell orchestra" made music.

How Millionaires Helped Start the Art Museum

It has been said that art follows money, and a century ago Cleveland had money for a museum—money from families whose New England Yankee forebears hadcome penniless to the city in the 19th century and founded iron, oil, coal, and real estate fortunes. Four of these millionaires were founders of the Museum of Art: John Huntington, Horace Kelley, Hinman Hurlbut and J.H. Wade II.

They weren't tycoons on the scale of Andrew Carnegie or John D. Rockefeller, but they were community movers and shakers. They were also fiercely independent men who didn't always let the right hand know what the left hand was doing.

For example, Huntington, Kelley and Hurlbut made bequests for an art museum without telling each other; Wade gave the 4 acres on which it now stands. There could have been a museum by 1892, but the John Huntington Art and Polytechnic Trust and Kelley Foundation were each set up so that it was legally impossible to join them, and a good part of the Hurlbut Fund money was spent by his widow before her death. Much legal maneuvering took place before everything was joined together as the Cleveland Museum of Art in 1913. What was left of the Hurlbut Fund was used to buy pictures and other art objects and their collection came to the museum.

A statement by the art museum's board in 1910, six years before opening, gives you some idea of why Cleveland ended up with a great and different museum: It wanted to hire a director who would "create an art interest in the community. A building filled with art objects is not necessarily a successful museum of art. A community must be interested and its active cooperation secured. A campaign of education should be carried on simultaneously with the growth of the institution."

With this mandate, when the project was only a hole in the ground with a fence around it, Frederick Whiting, a social worker,

John Huntington created the John Huntington Art
and Polytechnic Trust, a bequest that later would
help start the Cleveland Museum of Art.
(Cleveland Public Library)

was hired as the first director. And not surprisingly, he looked at the museum from a social worker's viewpoint. Whiting wanted the whole community to be served—children, blue-collar, industrialist—everyone was welcome; no one would question how you dressed, talked or how you pronounced your name.

Whiting saw the museum as a teaching institution as well as an artistic storehouse. He recommended that the museum "should strive for a happy medium between the restlessness which goes with constantly changing exhibitions and the monotony of a comparatively small building filled with permanently installed exhibits." His monthly Bulletin is still going strong today; he foreshadowed the annual "May Show" by recommending an exhibition by Ohio artists as early as 1914, and above all, encouraged education—lectures, children's classes, college and school cooperation.

When the striking new Beaux-Arts building opened June 6, 1916, it became the model for a generation of art museums. It was the first in the nation built to handle all aspects of the growing museum profession—acquisitions, registration, storage, photography, exhibition, education. There was just one little problem— it had practically no permanent collection, and very little money with which to acquire one. With what money it had, it bought John Singleton Copley's "Portrait of Mrs. Greene," in line with a policy of collecting important American painters. (Also, it was inexpensive.)

Then there were 122 American paintings from the Hurlbut collection, and Delia Holden's beloved collection of "Italian primitives" which she gave to the museum following Liberty Holden's death. Not much for openers, but the museum opened with what retired director Evan Turner called "an act of reasoned courage."

There was plenty of social, political and entertainment action going on in the city that June weekend. The Cleveland Grays, with its membership of leading businessmen, was scrambling all over Bedford Park in mock war games in case they were called up for duty with Gen. John J. Pershing in Mexico; the Ziegfeld Follies was playing at the Opera House with Will Rogers, Bert Williams, and "Funny Girl" Fanny Brice; the Cleveland Orchestra had picked a director, and the Play House company had been founded.

The art museum opening was a smash, with 2,000 excited Clevelanders, 40 representatives of art institutions from all over the country, and lots of hype from the local newspapers, the Leader, the Topics and The Plain Dealer, the latter declaring it "the beginning of an era in the city's history."

Cleveland had been very late with its museum.

Cincinnati the grande dame of the state, had opened its museum in 1886; Toledo and Columbus were up and operating, and Dayton was almost ready to go.

Late or not, by the end of the art exhibition, the Cleveland Museum of Art had logged more than 191,500 visitors; by the end of the first full year, 376,000.

Not bad for the husky new kid on the block.

World War I Brings Many Changes: Patriotic Excitement, Racial Hostility

A lot of things ended and a lot of things began anew in Cleveland when America was swept into World War I in 1917.

The city's last great progressive mayor, Newton Baker, was now secretary of war under President Woodrow Wilson, and the spirit of idealism of the Tom Johnson mayoral days would sputter and almost die out under his successors.

But the nation and city were still caught up in the patriotic excitement as the war began. There were parades, rallies, war-bond drives, rationing programs, war gardens. Cleveland's young men volunteered to go "Over There" and finish off the Kaiser's legions. Forty-one thousand would leave from the lakefront Union Depot to serve in the war.

The war and immigration laws had almost ended large-scale European immigration to the city. But Cleveland's booming war factories needed workers, so recruiting agents were sent to the poverty-stricken rural South. Their efforts were so successful that the mass movement of blacks into Northern cities and Cleveland became known as the Great Migration.

What had been a well-integrated black population of 8,500 in the city in 1910 grew to almost 35,000 by 1920, and 72,000 a decade later. "There is no mistaking what is going on, it is a regular Exodus," said the Cleveland Advocate, a black newspaper, in 1917.

It certainly was an exodus, but for black families the only thing that came free in the Promised Land was racial hostility.

Now, what had been considered the most liberal city in the Midwest in terms of race relations was going to experience conflict and friction in employment and education; discrimination against blacks in restaurants, theaters, hospitals, trains, department stores and public schools became common.

John Philip Sousa's Band (the Great Lakes Naval Station Band) marches
on Superior Ave. between Public Square and E. 6th St. during a
WWI Liberty Loan drive. *(CSU)*

But rural Southern blacks, with no education or urban experience, continued to pour into the East Side.

Historian Carol Poh Miller reports that boarding and rooming
houses were packed. Single-family, eight-room houses were divided
into "suites" with five or six families crowded in, using one bath-
room. Each unit rented for what the whole house had rented for
before.

Politicians in both parties sometimes played very dangerous
games with the rising white hostility and fear. Profesor Kenneth
Kusmer tells of the state chairman of the Democratic Party, William
Finley, in 1917, claiming that the Ohio GOP was assisting in the
"colonization" of thousands of traditionally Republican black mi-
grants for the purpose of increasing the Republican vote—a claim
that one year later was one of the causes of a notoriously bloody
race riot in East St. Louis, Mo.

Two newspapers, the News and the Leader, stirred things up
by prejudiced articles and remarks; the movie "Birth of a Nation"
played to sell-out crowds.

And there was more than racial hostility in the air after the war. Fear of "Red Bolshevism" was sweeping the country and thousands of suspects were jailed. On May 1, 1919, Socialist and trade unionist groups marched on Public Square to celebrate May Day, and to protest the jailing of Socialist leader Eugene Debs. They carried red flags and were taunted by spectators. A riot broke out, and police and Army troops had to break it up. Two people were killed, 40 injured and 116 arrested.

Cleveland's economic boom, though, continued during the "Roaring '20s." Auto and auto parts factories employed thousands of workers, and fat payrolls helped tamp down social unrest. As many as 150 labor unions, mostly AFL, were scattered throughout the city, the largest representing railroad workers.

With the war over, Americans loosened up; the pursuit of fun and profit were becoming the national pastime. Playhouse Square and Doan's Corners at Euclid Ave. and E. 105th St. were filled with new theaters. Young people danced the Charleston, and taxi drivers had hot market tips.

Middle-class people were using rapid transit lines and autos to flee the old ethnic neighborhoods—Warszawa, Dutch Hill, Kuba and the Angle were emptying out in favor of Farfield Heights, Parma, Cleveland Heights and Shaker Heights. Russian Jews and Italians were moving further east. Old, elegant Euclid Ave. mansions were being abandoned as used car lots moved in. Everything was changing. And then, on a late October day in 1929, everything would change again—forever!

Brothers Plant Seed for Modern Cleveland

The Van Sweringen brothers of Cleveland have been called a lot of things, both good and bad.

George Condon, the Cleveland historian, says, "They were the builders of modern Cleveland." Others blame them for the collapse of local banks during the Great Depression; this caused such a trauma that local financiers never quite got over it, and in turn wouldn't risk any venture capital for new projects that might have arrested the city's decline during the 1970s and '80s.

Then there were the charges of racial and religious prejudice—open appeals to "escape the commercial and social encroachments of the city." Translated, this meant getting away from blacks, Catholics and Jews.

Oris, (or O.P. as he was known) was the older brother, and Mantis (or M.J.) was two years younger; they were reclusive, painfully shy, never married, had no children, nor ever, as far as is known, had an affair with anything other than a dollar. For all intents and purposes, they might have been one person. They lived together and never seemed to need friends or family—just each other.

They were descended from very early Dutch forebears, and their father had dropped the "Van" from his name; the brothers put it back in after they almost went belly up selling real estate in Lakewood around the turn of the century. It was the East Side that turned out to be the gold mine the brothers had been looking for, specifically, North Park Blvd. in Cleveland Heights. Here home buyers could get away from those pushy immigrants who were pouring into Cleveland from Eastern Europe; away from the blacks who were coming up from the South in droves; and away from the commercial blight that was destroying the livability of posh Euclid Ave.

Selling beautiful homes on North Park Blvd. led naturally to doing the same thing further out in the Heights on Fairmount Blvd. Here the key was persuading the Cleveland Railway Co. to extend its tracks and service to the Van Sweringens' new subdivision.

Mantis Van Sweringen (left) and Oris Van Sweringen
(right), the reclusive bachelor brothers who developed
Shaker Heights. *(CSU)*

But the brothers had something else in mind, perhaps from the start of their careers—the 1,366 acres of the old North Union Shaker Colony, a deserted ruin of grist mills, stone quarries, community buildings and small lakes. It was on this once sacred land, the Valley of God's Pleasure, that the Van Sweringens would begin in 1905 to create the most famous and affluent suburb in America, Shaker Heights, by buying the land from a Buffalo syndicate for $1 million.

But there was a problem: In 1906, even wealthy people who owned autos didn't use them to commute to work in the city, and there was no public transportation for the six miles from Shaker Village to downtown Cleveland. The Cleveland Railway Co. wanted no part of extending its transit lines any further.

Well, nobody ever accused the Van Sweringens of lacking courage. They decided to build their own railroad, and with the blissful ignorance of amateurs began acquiring the right-of-way down the Kingsbury Run ravine to Cleveland. Four of the needed six miles fell into place, but the last two vital miles to downtown were owned by the New York Central's Nickel Plate road—and it wouldn't sell.

Again, with luck, the Interstate Commerce Commission ruled that the NYC had to sell the road—the whole 539-mile road, that is—and the Van Sweringens had to raise $8.5 million on top of their already heavy debt load if they wanted the whole railroad!

Incredibly, and it can only be explained by the free-wheeling, unregulated times, the Van Sweringens floated stock in a new company, bought the Nickel Plate, and in 1916, began to build their own rail line from Shaker Village to Cleveland.

Now came the big fight. They needed one final piece to put into place the grand mosaic of their design: a new terminal on the southwest side of Public Square, right where their tracks came in; one that would replace their own grimy little station right in the heart of Cleveland's high-crime area. Never mind that all six of the major railroads and a public referendum in 1915 had agreed on a new lakefront depot as part of the famous Group Plan. Never mind that Euclid Ave. merchants, the Pennsylvania Railroad and political reformers wanted the lakefront site—the Van Sweringens wanted their corner of the square for the new Union Terminal.

And in 1919, there was a new referendum, with the brothers campaigning on the basis of cleaning up crime and creating jobs. The Van Sweringens won their final round.

Now this odd couple would proceed to put Cleveland on the national map.

Depression Derailed
Van Sweringen Express

Those two masters of the game of real estate, the Van Sweringen brothers of Cleveland, had just made their greatest coup, winning a referendum in 1919 that gave them development rights for their Union Terminal complex on the southwest corner of Public Square.

Against all odds and seeming common sense, they had first overpaid for the old Shaker North Union Colony acreage; then, in order to make the area accessible to future home buyers, acquired the Nickle Plate Railroad, 539 miles long, to get a vital two miles for their own transit line over its right-of-way from their Shaker Village development to downtown Cleveland. Now, the final piece in the jigsaw puzzle was in place, and the work started, work that would take 11 years and $200 million.

By 1920, 35 acres of historic old Cleveland were being cleared west from Public Square down the hill to the river. Something was gained and something was lost. Squalid, disease-ridden hovels fell to the wrecker's ball; so did some landmark old inns and restaurants. Fifteen thousand people were displaced from their homes—as rundown and riddled with crime as the area was, it was home to them.

The crowning jewel of the complex was the 52-story Terminal Tower; next to it was Higbee's Department Store; behind it was a brand-new street with two more high-rise office buildings. But underneath the tower was what it was all about, because here all the major railroads, except the Pennsylvania converged. This was a time when railroads seemed all-powerful, the industry that legendary robber barons like Jay Gould, Commodore Vanderbilt, and Leland Stanford had made part of the American industrial fabric. Nobody could have foreseen the end of their dominance of passenger travel within a relatively few years.

As for Shaker Village, that exclusive community had succeeded beyond even the Van Sweringen brothers' wildest dreams! They had added an average of 300 new, expensive homes each year from

Completed in 1927, the Terminal Tower was the tallest
building in the United States outside of New York until
1927. *(Cleveland Public Library)*

1919 to 1929, and the population had gone from 1,700 to 15,500 in
the same time. In 1931, it became a city and changed its name to
Shaker Heights.

And those 1,366 acres of Shaker land that the Van Sweringens
had bought from a Buffalo syndicate for $1 million was now valued
at $80 million.

Shaker Village seems to have been among the first planned suburban communities in the country. And its very restrictions were
what made it so attractive to so many affluent buyers. In the '20s
and '30s, you weren't permitted to buy or resell a house until you
got permission from all the neighbors, plus that of the Van Sweringen Co. The latter had to approve the architect, the paint colors,
even the realtors!

There were 99-year deed restrictions that effectively kept out Jews, Catholics and blacks until after World War II. The Van Sweringens persuaded Cleveland's University School to relocate in Shaker, and they were soon followed by Hathaway Brown and Laurel School. It was typical of Oris O. and Mantis J. Van Sweringen that after acquiring the whole Nickle Plate Railroad, almost as an afterthought, they set about buying 24 more railroads to the tune of 27,000 miles of trackage, and that led to being involved with more than 200 other companies including real estate, traction and coal interests that may have had some $4 billion dollars of assets, according to historian George Condon.

Had success gone to the heads of the two shy, reclusive bachelors?

Hardly! On June 28, 1930, Terminal Tower and the Union Terminal were to be dedicated with an immense party of prominent Clevelanders and guests from all over the country. After all, it was the greatest city center complex that had ever been built up to that point. (Rockefeller Center was several years away.) But O.P. and M.J. Van Sweringen weren't there—they stayed home and listened to the celebration on the radio.

But not even the Van Sweringens could have foreseen the disaster that the Great Depression would create. Railroad revenues plunged, Shaker real estate was going for a song—if it went at all. And the Van Sweringens were into two local banks for a lot of loans, loans that were called and the collateral lost. Even a huge loan from the J.P. Morgan bank wasn't enough to bail them out, and at the end of September 1935, at an auction of their assets, several entrepreneurs picked up some $3 billion of assets for a little over $3 million.

The two local banks who had loaned the Van Sweringens all that money never re-opened their doors, and there are Clevelanders to this day who feel that their collapse, caused by the Van Sweringens' defaulted loans, was such a devastating financial and psychological blow to this area that only now it has really begun to recover.

From the Roaring '20s to the Great Depression, the Van Sweringens led the rise and fall of a great city.

Depression, Recovery in Hard-Hit Cleveland

Roosevelt's 'New Deal' Helped Build Landmarks, City's Spirit After Stockmarket Crash

Cleveland didn't get much time to celebrate the opening of the Union Terminal Tower complex on June 28, 1930.

On the surface, everything looked fine. The complex looked out on new office buildings, newly completed buildings of Tom Johnson's famous Group Plan like the Public Auditorium and the Public Library. The Board of Education building and the Stadium were on the way.

Cleveland's city manager, William Hopkins, had given his name to the new Municipal Airport. Lakewood, East Cleveland, Cleveland Heights and Shaker Heights, were booming as the children of the city's foreign-born immigrants fled to the suburbs, leaving their old ethnic neighborhoods behind.

But the stock market crash of Oct. 29, 1929, "Black Tuesday," had started the country and city on an irreversible downhill slide. Cleveland—the nation's sixth largest city with more than 900,000 people, and Cuyahoga County, at 1,200,000 the third largest metropolitan area, following only New York and Chicago—would be the hardest-hit area in the country. This industrial powerhouse slowed to a crawl as steel mills, foundries, shipyards, railroads and refineries closed their doors.

Cleveland went from 41,000 unemployed in April 1930, to 100,000 by January 1931—one-third of the city's workers. City and county were overwhelmed with direct demands for relief just as their tax revenues were dropping.

President Franklin Roosevelt's "New Deal" stepped into the breach with the famous alphabet agencies such as the Civil Works Administration (CWA), and the much-maligned WPA (Work Progress Administration). To those many thousands who had stood in line at soup kitchens or sold apples on street corners, it was their only safety net.

These agencies built the Main Avenue Bridge, the Stadium, Memorial Shoreway (from E. 9th St. to Gordon Park), schools, streets, sewers, waterworks, and developed the city's park system into the Cleveland Metroparks system, "a generation ahead of schedule."

WPA art was derided, but artists like William Somers would turn out paintings and murals that would justify the expenditure to later generations. Cleveland used federal money to build the first public housing in the nation, starting Cedar-Central, Outhwaite Homes and Lakeview Terrace in 1935. But all the money pumped into the economy in those years was only a fraction of the normal wages and salaries lost.

The ugly, desperate mood of the city was lifted somewhat in 1936 when local business leaders opened the Great Lakes Exposition, celebrating the industry and culture of the surrounding area, stating in their prospectus, "Cleveland has for several years been so depressed by adverse circumstances that a forward-looking enterprise is needed to revive the sagging spirit of civic pride that formerly characterized the city."

Portions of the lakefront were filled in and slums were cleared from the Stadium to E. 20th St., and for two years, hundreds of thousands of visitors stolled down the Avenue of the Presidents to see science, engineering and art exhibits—or, for a little fun, Billy Rose's Aquacade starring Eleanor Holm and Johnny "Tarzan" Weissmuller. Then there was Sally Rand with her famous fan dance.

In June, 10,000 Republican delegates marched down Euclid Ave. during the presidential nominating convention. They eventually picked Gov. Alf Landon of Kansas to be the sacrificial lamb against FDR.

It was grand year for sports, too. That August, black track star Jesse Owens, graduate of East Technical High School and Ohio State University, was greeted by thousands as he returned from the Olympics in Berlin where he had won three gold medals and was part of the 400-meter relay team to win a fourth medal to the disgust of dictator Adolf Hitler.

Then, on Aug. 23, a 17-year-old rookie pitcher named Bob Feller started for the Indians and struck out 15 St. Louis Browns, one short of the American League record. Three weeks later, the day the Expo recorded its 3 millionth visitor, he struck out 17 of Connie Mack's Philadelphia Athletics. For those who couldn't get into the ballpark, there was the play-by-play on the radio from Pinky Hunter and Jack Graney.

In 1937, Republic Steel fought union organizers at its Cleveland and Youngstown plants; one was killed and 60 injured in the city until the National Guard took over.

Eventually, rearmament and World War II would lead to the economic revival of the area—but the Depression generation would forever be scarred with the fear and insecurity of those days.

Ness, a Mr. Clean Cleveland Desperately Needed

Cleveland's own G-Man, Eliot Ness, came to town in the summer of 1934 as head of the Treasury Department's Alcohol Tax Unit. He had achieved celebrity as the chief of a special Justice Department task force that had literally battered down the doors of Al Capone's breweries and warehouses in Chicago during Prohibition, but it would be many years later, long after Ness was dead, before a book and TV would make him into a near-mythical lawman.

Ness had always given credit for jailing Capone to the undercover work of the IRS, but he was symbolic of the new breed of enforcement officer: college-educated, smart, and incorruptible— "untouchable" as he became known for spurning constant bribe offers from Capone.

Cleveland had a new mayor, Harold Burton, who, when he couldn't get the Republican Party's endorsement, ran as an independent Republican and won. Burton appointed the 32-year-old Ness as his safety director in charge of a thoroughly demoralized force of 2,400 policemen and firemen.

Times had changed since Cleveland's men in blue were the recognized model for the country under Mayor Tom Johnson; now, with the worst depression in history in full bloom, there were hundreds of homeless people, panhandlers, prostitutes and robbers; gambling was wide open, labor extortion common, the police rackets at full blast. Cops looked and acted the way they felt—slovenly and unkempt; sometimes they were informants and even enforcers for mob figures.

In December 1935, author Steven Nickel quoted Ness as telling the Cleveland Advertising Club, "In any city where corrpution continues, it follows that some officers are playing ball with the underworld. If town officials are committed to a program of 'protection,' police work becomes exceedingly difficult, and the officer on the beat, being discouraged from his duty, decides it is best to see as little crime as possible."

Eliot Ness (far right) meets with Cleveland mayor Frank Laushe (far left) and Indiana governor Paul V. McNutt. Ness moved to town in 1934 with the goal of cleaning up the police department and ridding the city of crime. *(Cleveland Public Library)*

Ness went on to explain that while he personally wasn't against gambling, profits from illegal gambling opened the door to drug dealing, prostitution and union racketeering.

Quite a mouthful for a young man whom many locals considered not tough enough to be a top cop, with his college-boy good looks, university education and low-key manner. They began to believe him when he transferred 122 policemen, including a captain and 27 lieutenants, and replaced the head of the detective bureau.

Ness captured Cleveland's affection when he made a flamboyant and courageous raid on the Harvard Club in Newburg Heights, a notorious gambling club operating openly with police protection, one month after his appointment as safety director. He had been called in by the county prosecutor even though the club was out of the city limits, and moved against it as a private citizen, accompanied by police and his newspaper reporter friends.

Now, with the city solidly behind him, Ness put together a team of volunteer detectives and police—Cleveland's own group of "Un-touchables"—and went after corruption in the police force. He used wiretaps, informers, subpoenaed bank accounts; the same tools of the trade he had used against Al Capone in Chicago. Grand jury indictments, trials and convictions followed.

Later, juries would send labor extortionists to jail, leading to anti-union charges against Ness. The AFL investigated and decided that Ness was only against labor racketeering.

He instituted a professional training program for police and reformed the traffic division leading to Cleveland being rated the safest city in the United States by the National Safety Council.

Many evenings, on his own time, he met with youth gang leaders and social workers. He fought to get city funding of playgrounds and basketball courts for Cleveland's youth: "Keep them off the streets and keep them busy. It's much better to spend a lot of time and money . . . keeping them straight than it is to spend even more time and money catching them in the wrong and then trying to set them straight."

As a result of his programs, there was an 80 percent drop in juvenile delinquency.

Then, a much greater evil than corruption or organized crime struck: a serial killer—the man the media would call the Cleveland Butcher—who left pieces of corpses scattered about.

Even Ness Can't Catch Vicious 'Torso Murderer'

When Mayor Harold Burton appointed Eliot Ness Cleveland's safety director in 1935, it was with the idea of cleaning up the city's notorious organized crime, and the police and political corruption that permitted it to flourish. And they were successful.

Citizens were now cooperating with the police, phoning in leads, offering to testify against hoodlums. Grand juries were returning indictments by the score.

But a totally different kind of criminal was already operating in Cleveland: a serial killer who would be dubbed by the media the "Torso Murderer," the "Cleveland Butcher" or the "Mad Butcher of Kingsbury Run".

In September 1935, before the Ness appointment, two corpses had been found in Kingsbury Run, decapitated, emasculated and dismembered. Homicide detectives had identified one man as Edward Andrassy, a small-time hoodlum with a lot of enemies; the other man was never identified. Detectives ran down scores of leads, but nothing panned out.

A few months later, another butchered body turned up in an alley off E. 20th St.; this time it was a woman—Flo Polillo—a prostitute with a long string of aliases, lovers, husbands and arrests for drunkenness and solicitation.

Then, on June 5, three days before the Republican National Convention was to open in the city, two kids discovered a head in Kingsbury Run, near the transit tracks that ran under the Kinsman Rd. bridge; the rest of the body was found the next day.

On the same warm Sunday afternoon in September 1936 on which Cleveland Indians pitcher Bob Feller registered 17 strikeouts against the Philadelphia Athletics, more than 5,000 people gathered around a polluted pond in the Run to watch a professional diver, hired by the city, search for the arms and legs of another victim of the "Butcher"—at least the sixth, more likely the eighth.

Eliot Ness questions a group of shantytown residents, searching for a lead in the Torso Murder case. *(CSU)*

Detectives were beginning to see the pattern: decapitation, dismemberment and sexual mutilation, performed skillfully by a very strong killer.

But the police didn't want to panic the public. When a detective told a reporter that there was "a maniac with a lust to kill" loose in the city, according to author Steven Nickel, he was immediately taken off the case. But the newspapers were beginning to sense trouble, and that worried Mayor Burton, who in turn pressured Ness to get personally involved. Ness told reporters, "I want to see this psycho caught. I'm going to do all I can to aid in the investigation."

At the Great Lakes Exposition that year, Ness organized a police exhibit featuring all the latest in criminology techniques—and a death mask of one of the unidentified victims found in Kingsbury Run.

Anyone with information was urged to phone the police. Many thousands of visitors would see this display in coming months, but nobody knew who he was, or why the "Torso Killer" had picked him to be one of his victims.

Ness had his police chief assign his two top homicide detectives full time to the case, Peter Merylo and his partner, Martin Zalewski. At night, after the other detectives went home, the partners would walk the streets of the "Roaring Third" precinct, questioning prostitutes, bartenders, drug addicts and saloon customers. Some nights they dressed as tramps and slept in the hobo jungles of the Flats, taking turns watching over each other sleeping, hoping to lure the mad killer with the butcher knives. Scores of weird, often violent suspects were turned up—but none was the one the police were looking for.

By the summer of 1938, victims No. 11 and No. 12 had been found—a man and a woman, completely dismembered. As usual, fingerprints and dental checks hadn't even led to their identification, much less to the killer. Front-page editorials by The Plain Dealer and the Press were demanding action. The latter said: "Unusual means must be taken to bring the detection of one of the most horrible killers in criminal history."

Mayor Burton's political opponent had almost beaten him for re-election the previous November by talking about the "Ness-Burton failure to solve the horrible 'Torso' crimes." What was needed, he said, was a local lawman as safety director, not "a G-Man from Chicago."

Driven by anger, frustration and newspaper criticism, on a hot August night Eliot Ness launched a raid on the hobo jungles of the Flats in the hope of turning up some evidence that would nail the "Mad Butcher." Ness, lawmen and firemen moved in with fire-trucks, floodlights, clubs and axes, rounding up the ragged tramps who lived there. Then the miserable shacks were destroyed. The end result was only more newspaper criticism.

Several years later, with one of greatest mass murderers in history, Adolf Hitler, marching in Europe, the public began losing interest in the case.

And the "Cleveland Butcher"? Like Jack the Ripper before him, he vanished into the fog of the night—leaving only a terrible myth.

WWII Brought Myriad Changes to Cleveland

It was time for war. The Japanese attack on Pearl Harbor on Dec. 7, 1941, had united a deeply split country as nothing else could have possibly done. Now there were no more neutrals, interventionists or America Firsters; no more Labor vs. Industry; no more Great Depression.

Where there had once been hundreds of men in line for any few available jobs that opened up, there were now manpower shortages created by the draft and the huge government war orders pouring into Cleveland's industrial complex. General Electric, TRW, Parker-Hannifin, and hundreds of subcontractors were making aircraft parts, tanks, trucks, artillery, cartridge cases, bombs, binoculars and telescopes. NASA got its start in 1943, and what is now the giant International Exposition Center next to Cleveland Hopkins International Airport was built by Fisher Body to produce tanks. Cleveland companies made the machines that made the war materials, made the paint that covered them.

Thousands of women who had never worked before were suddenly in demand for production lines. "Rosie the Riveter" was a real person who now could support her family on the $40-$45 a week that she made; or she could get that kind of money as a stenographer. A city that had seemed flat on its back just a few years earlier was climbing to new economic heights, as part of Franklin Delano Roosevelt's "Arsenal of Democracy."

Poor rural blacks repeated their World War I exodus from the South up to the city with those high-paying jobs, almost doubling their numbers from 85,000 in 1940 to 148,000 in 1950. Thousands of Appalachian whites and Puerto Ricans settled on the near West Side.

The downside for the area, as in all the nation's wars, was the lengthening list of casualties of Cleveland's young men posted in Public Square. The price was heavy.

Frank Lausche, of Slovenian descent, was the wartime mayor of

The V-J Day celebration at E. 9th St. and Euclid Ave. *(Cleveland Public Library)*

Cleveland. Old-line conservative citizens had trouble pronouncing his name, but they liked his tight-fisted spending policies; so would the rest of the state when he became governor in 1945 and then was elected to the U.S. Senate.

The war stopped new home construction for four years, but far-sighted people could see ahead to what was likely to happen after it was over. As early as 1941, according to historians Carol Poh Miller and Robert Wheeler, the Chamber of Commerce stated: "It is evident that most people who live in Cleveland are anxious to move to the suburbs—experience has shown that if their economic status permits, the majority of Clevelanders prefer to live outside the central area." And why was this?: Crime, congestion, environmental factors, and the key words: "proximity of races having a depreciatory effect on values."

Racial tensions were heightening when the Welfare Federation began a two-year study in 1943 of the racial and economic conditions in the black neighborhoods. Frank Lausche that same year set up a committee of white and black community activists to work toward eradicating discrimination in employment, housing and public accommodations. By 1945, this would become the Community Relations Board; its mission: "To promote amicable relations among the racial and cultural groups within the community."

And again, in 1943, the mayor organized the Postwar Planning Council to plan for the day when those huge war orders would dry up, and all those thousands of GIs would be coming home, looking for homes and jobs—pretty farsighted for a time when most people were thinking only of when—and if—their sons, husbands, and daughters were coming home!

The aim of the council was, in the mayor's words: "not only to build the bridge from war to peacetime production but also to lay plans for making Cleveland's industrial advantages so patent that we can keep all of the industries we have and attract new ones."

By the time of the city's 150th birthday in 1946, with the war over, optimism prevailed. a New York Times writer said, "Clevelanders display exuberant enthusiasm for their town and their way of life such as you don't recall ever noting in any city east of the Alleghenies. . . ."

Was Cleveland really "the Best Location in the Nation?"

Or was trouble coming to Forest City?

Baseball Wisdom

Sport Mirrors Ups And Downs of Town Since First Pro Forest City Team's Game

It's been said that baseball is a faithful American mirror: In it we see ourselves, our times, understated, caught unawares . . .

It's the eighth inning of the first game of the 1954 World Series. Sal Maglie of the New York Giants and Bob Lemon of the Cleveland Indians are locked in a 2-2 pitching duel at the Polo Grounds in New York.

Cleveland is the favorite of two-thirds of the sportswriters in the country; the Indians have pitching and power hitting, have set an American League record of 111 wins. Larry Doby led the AL with 32 homers and 126 RBIs, Al Rosen had 24 homers and 102 RBIs, Vic Wertz is a slugger, second baseman Bobby Avila led the league with a .341 batting average. Bob Lemon and Early Wynn each won 23 games, Mike Garcia, 19; aging Bob Feller, his famed fastball replaced with slow curves, was 13-3; the bullpen was strong.

Doby, the first black ballplayer in the AL, walks to lead off the inning. Rosen follows with a single, bringing up Wertz, who has already had three hits against Maglie. Giants manager Leo Durocher brings in left-hander Don Liddle to pitch to Wertz.

There hadn't been many winning Cleveland baseball teams since that first pro game by the Forest City team in 1869, at the dawn of the Industrial Age. Clevelanders got used to disappointment early; they lost that one 25-6 to Cincinnati. Finally, after many ups and downs (mostly downs), the tough, scrappy Cleveland Spiders, with their player-manager Patsy Tebeau, met the Baltimore Orioles in 1895 for the Temple Cup playoffs—the World Series of the day.

The first three games were to be played in League Park and crowds of 12,500 turned out to see their heroes win all three, with lengendary pitcher Cy Young accounting for two of the three wins.

Larry Doby became the first African-American player in the American League when he signed with the Indians in 1947. *(Cleveland Public Library)*

Local fans helped the home team by bombarding the visitors with food, cans, anything they could throw.

When the team moved on to Baltimore to play the next three games, the Baltimore fans pelted the players with rotten eggs and vegetables.

Even when the Spiders lost the first game, the assault continued against the players in their horse-drawn bus all the way back to their hotel. "The Cleveland players had to sprawl flat on the floor of the bus to escape serious injury," reported The Plain Dealer.

But Cy Young and the Spiders weren't cowed by this hooliganism. The next afternoon, Cy "Old Tuscarawas" Young beat them for the third time, and that gave the series to Cleveland, 4-1. The Plain Dealer reporter in his dispatch said, "The Champions' pennant is all smeared with mud. The Orioles kept up the clip for a while, but then the streaks of 'yellow' showed, and it was all over."

Big Vic Wertz smacks Liddle's first pitch to right centerfield; it rises in a beautiful arc—a sure home run in any field other than the Polo Grounds where the centerfield fence is 460 feet.

Then after a downhill slide and several years out of pro baseball, came years of struggling in the new American League until another great player-manager, Tris Speaker, led a Cleveland team to victory in a nine-game World Series against the Brooklyn Dodgers in 1920. The team and the city had made a good start in the Roaring '20s.

Willie Mays is running, sprinting flatout in centerfield; he turns his back on the ball.

No winning dynasty was created by the 1920 team, however. The 17-year-old pitcher, Bob Feller, would help pack the new Stadium for 20 years—from 1936 to 1956—with fans coming from Detroit, Toledo and Pittsburgh to see him pitch.

Then Bill Veeck came to town in 1946 and put together a team that would beat the Boston Braves in the Series of 1948. He was a flamboyant, colorful showman who fit the town's postwar buoyancy.

Mays reaches over his left shoulder with his glove: He makes "The Catch!" The Giants go on to win the first game with a pop-fly home run and make a four-game sweep of the 1954 World Series. Cleveland hearts sink.

And the city—what did the future hold for it? Well, another famous Cleveland pitcher, Satchel Paige, once said: "Don't look back. Something might be gaining on you."

City Meets Challenges
Right from Its Beginning

Cleveland Has Displayed an
Instinct for Survival

Cleveland's history really started when U.S. Army troops decisively defeated hostile Indian tribes at the Battle of Fallen Timbers, near present-day Toledo, Aug. 24, 1794. Out of this came a treaty that left the lands west of the Cuyahoga River in Indian hands, but confirmed Connecticut's claims to the land east of the river up to the Pennsylvania line—its Western Reserve.

Connecticut investors formed the Connecticut Land Co. and promptly bought all 3 million acres for $1,200,000. They sent their chief surveyor and investor, Gen. Moses Cleaveland, to lay out a town in a typical real-estate venture—buy cheap and sell high.

Cleaveland and his 50-man party arrived at the mouth of the Cuyahoga July 22, 1796—and departed for good after three months, leaving only a few people to face the winter winds and the malarial mosquitoes of summer that swarmed up from the swampy, sandbar choked river mouth.

New settlers came in, looked, and fled the malaria, east to Doan's Corners, south to Newburg Heights, or west of the river, where Indian claims were again "extinguished" in 1804.

A few hundred men and women hung on through the War of 1812, grazing their pigs and cows on Public Square, until Commodore Perry's victory at the Battle of Lake Erie lifted the British/Indian threat to the region.

The struggling little hamlet of Cleveland then looked on jealously as Lorain, Sandusky, Painesville and Ashtabula grew and became prosperous ports.

But a Cleveland politician named Alfred Kelley saw to it that the state of Ohio made Cleveland the northern terminus of the Ohio Canal in 1825.

In a few years, Ohio's farmers could ship their produce to the

East via Cleveland, and receive all manner of industrial products by the same route. A hustling little center of commerce grew up along the Flats: merchants, shippers, small industries.

Kelley again shoved Cleveland into the future, building its first railroad: his locomotive chugged into town in February 1851 at a speedy 25 mph. Coal and limestone would soon be carried here, and lake steamers would drop off iron and copper ores for Cleveland's mills and foundries.

The Civil War accelerated the industrial expansion, and thanks to the oil strike in western Pennsylvania, 30 refineries made Cleveland an oil boomtown with smog, river pollution and riches—the later mostly going to a ruthless young man named John D. Rockefeller whose Standard Oil Trust would come to dominate the refining business by 1882.

The Industrial Age hurtled in as Eastern European immigrants poured into the city, often crowding into disease-ridden tenements and shacks, creating their own neighborhoods based on family, religion and language. The foundries, rolling mills, shipbuilding yards and machine shops employed the men; women worked as domestics, waitresses and in the textile and paint industries. Labor unions fought—sometimes violently—for their share of the industrial pie.

The new millionaires vied with one another to build showy mansions on Euclid Ave. One, Tom Johnson, became mayor in 1901, and in four terms made Cleveland internationally famous for progressive politics: prison reform, public health programs, municipal lighting, low-priced street railways, efficient police, a downtown Group Plan.

Other men and women poured their time and money back into the community creating cultural institutions like the Cleveland Museum of Art, Severance Hall and the Cleveland Orchestra, the Public Library, and theaters. Their settlement houses for immigrants and their organized charitable fund raising became models for the country.

Southern, rural blacks were recruited to fill the city's industrial jobs during and after World War I. Poor families were crammed into overpriced, single-family homes as whites fled to the new suburbs, like Parma, Brooklyn and Lyndhurst.

During the Great Depression, the city slowed to a crawl during the 1930s, with only New Deal agencies like the Works Progress Administration standing between the unemployed and starvation.

World War II brought high casualties to the city's young men; but also brought an armaments boom that masked urban decay for 10 more years. Successive city administrations faced white flight to the suburbs, crime, pollution, racial tensions, loss of tax base.

City fortunes looked bleak after race riots in the 1960s. In 1978, under a young, populist mayor, Dennis Kucinich, Cleveland became the first major American city to go into default since the Great Depression.

Calamity accomplished what prosperity couldn't: The city's political and power structure united. The city's credit was restored; cooperation took the place of confrontation.

There were new educational and health facilities, a rebuilt downtown financial center, major new sports stadiums, great new entertainment, housing and retail complexes; an appreciation of the cultural institutions.

And, while there are still problems, the region has seen the return of something that's 200 years old today: Cleveland's spirit.

Cleveland On the Ebb

Flight to Suburbs, Riots Diminish City's Population, Prestige

Warszawsa, Dutch Hill, Kuba, Birdtown, The Angle, Whiskey Hill, Haymarket—half-forgotten names that were once everything to the immigrants who lived in these neighborhoods. The small businesses, schools, fraternal halls, churches and newspapers in these areas formed a mosaic that was spread across Cleveland based on family, religion and language.

In the 1950s these ethnic enclaves began coming unglued; the children of the immigrants didn't want any part of them. There was an exodus from the city to the new suburbs like Parma, Brooklyn, Lyndhurst, Mayfield Heights, Euclid. A low-interest FHA mortgage would buy a veteran a spanking new home with some grass, so why stay in the city with its crime, pollution and minorities moving into your ethnic neighborhood?

The big retailers were following their customers, going into huge, new suburban shopping malls. Industrial plants were being built close to highway access. And the old factories? They were either abandoned or the production was transferred to Texas or Taiwan, costing thousands of jobs.

Under President Dwight D. Eisenhower's administration, the 1956 Federal Highway Act was about to transform the country. Cleveland used federal money to knock down many older, stable neighborhoods, declaring them blighted, to make way for the new roads. Some 19,000 homes were demolished, resulting in a huge decline in property taxes.

The city had even more grandiose plans: the largest urban renewal in the nation using money from the Federal Housing Act of 1949 to demolish and clear over 6,000 acres of inner-city land. Thousands of poor, mostly black residents were sent packing with no provision for new housing or relocation funding. Packages of the cleared land were to be sold at a low cost to private developers who would then build middle-income housing.

Armed militant groups clashed with police and the National Guard in the 1968 Glenville shootout. *(CSU)*

More poor people were cleared out of the East Side to make room for commercial and industrial development. Those displaced were pushed into already overcrowded areas like Hough, Glenville and Mount Pleasant.

Realty agents called blockbusters were already hard at work in those areas, panicking white residents into selling out to them quickly for a song, then sub-dividing the homes and raising the rents. Hough went from a 95 percent white population in 1950 to 74 percent black 10 years later.

Only Erieview, that aging area northeast of E. 9th St., backed by the civic, political and corporate leadership of the city, attracted private developers to build office buildings, hotels and housing. To many, it seemed to signify the rebirth of the city.

And then, on the night of July 18, 1966, all those papered-over problems exploded into the Hough riots in the heart of the black ghetto.

Four days later, after four deaths and millions of dollars worth of damage, the National Guard was patroling the streets of a city that would never again look at itself complacently, never again think that new downtown bricks and mortar alone would keep the city great. Mayor Ralph Locher accurately described the riots as "a tragic day in the life of our city."

When Carl Stokes became mayor in 1967, the first black mayor of a large American city, it was hoped that he could reverse the decay—that he could, as a successful black politician, address the city's worst problem: race relations; that he could somehow handle a white, parochial, defensive police force.

Stokes was bright and articulate and had tremendous appeal not only to the black community, but to upper-middle-class whites who supported him financially.

And then came the Glenville shootout of July 23, 1968: an ambush of police by black militants that set the black ghetto on fire again and left 10 dead and dozens of wounded. When Stokes refused to let the police go into the area and arrest the militants for fear of worse violence, many in the white Cleveland community turned against him.

What was left of Stokes' suburban financial support evaporated further when it was learned that some money from Cleveland: NOW!—a major drive for cash contributions to the city improvements that had solicited everybody from corporations to school children—ended up in the pockets of the black militants involved in the battle.

After finishing a barely won second term, Carl Stokes left the city and politics for many years.

The city that once had led the way into the 20th century with vision and courage under Tom Johnson was now the nation's symbol for all that was going wrong in the country.

City with Pride

Others May Have Their Doubts, but Clevelanders Have Never Lost the Spirit

With Cleveland's official 200th birthday tomorrow, where does the city stand? We've been known by a lot of names: the "Comeback City of the '90s," the "Best Location in the Nation," and "The Mistake on the Lake." Which are we today?

If you watched late-night TV in the 1970s, there wouldn't have been much question about your answer then. The comedians laughed at a river that caught on fire. Then Mayor Ralph Perk set his hair on fire with an acetylene torch at a dedication ceremony, and his wife turned down a White House invitation from President Nixon—it was her bowling night. Plenty of good comic material there.

Some 20,000 people a year were leaving the city.

There had been a 40 percent drop in population from 1950 to 1980; neighborhoods had shuttered store fronts; heavy industry was pulling out for the Sunbelt or Asia; the once-famed public school system was collapsing.

Court-ordered busing led to even more suburban flight—by well-off blacks as well as whites.

Successive mayors from 1970 on were either unwilling or unable to raise taxes to cover shortfalls in expenditures. Even with federal aid covering one-third of the city budget, Mayor Perk had to borrow heavily against the city's credit and still sell off assets like the sewage-treatment facilities, the zoo, the transit system and the lakefront parks to regional authorities or the state.

When he proposed to sell off the Municipal Light Plant to the Cleveland Electric Illuminating Co., he left himself vulnerable to populist City Councilman Dennis Kucinich, who was elected mayor in 1977. At 32, he was the youngest big-city mayor in the United States.

The city's debt had become a tidal wave. Kucinich refused to sell Muny Light; (that and restoring neighborhoods had been his whole campaign plank). The banks, alienated by Kucinich and his Cabinet's confrontational approach, refused to roll over the debt, and the city went into default in December 1978, the first major American city to do so since the Great Depression.

Now Clevelanders of every income level were jolted into the realization that the city could be permanently finished. When former Lt. Gov. George Voinovich ran for mayor in 1980, the city was just waiting to be rescued. And Republican Voinovich would deal with the political reality of the council being run by a tough Democrat, George Forbes, by giving him some patronage in return for Forbes backing his political programs.

Now, at long last, cooperation took the place of confrontation; top corporate executives put the city's financial house in order; a city income tax was approved by voters who had regained a feeling of confidence in the future; the banks rolled the loans over; and the city emerged from default.

Happy ending, right? Well, this is really a tale of two cities, and the story isn't over for either.

One city has some of the most beautiful suburbs in America, where young professionals buy large homes for about one-third the price of the same home on the East or West coasts.

There are world-class cultural institutions in University Circle, first-class health and educational facilities, marvelous theaters and restaurants, ballet, dance and opera, even a baseball/basketball complex that's the talk of the sports world.

Downtown has been saved as a major financial center; Tower City and the Galleria have brought back major retailers; the Rock and Roll Hall of Fame and Musuem and the Great Lakes Science Center are up and running.

The Warehouse District has residential units, and the Flats are mobbed on weekend nights by young people.

And there's the other city; decaying neighborhoods, high unemployment, racial tension, crime, failing public schools.

Something intangible may make the crucial, winning difference for Cleveland: the city's spirit.

It was there on July 22, 1796, when Moses Cleaveland and his surveying crew form the Connecticut Land Co. headed into the mouth of the Cuyahoga River and set up shop.

In 1824, Harvey Rice, a future great Ohio educator, was rowed from his schooner at the entrance to Cleveland's harbor and spent the night at a log-cabin inn on Public Square.

The next morning he saw the muddy Square, cows and pigs wandering around, "begemmed with stumps, while near its center glowed its crowning jewel, a log courthouse. The eastern border of the Square was skirted by the native forest, which abounded in rabbits and squirrels."

The entire population at that time didn't exceed 400. But the town, even at that time, was proud of itself, and called itself "The Gem of the West!"

That's it. Those are the words—"Proud of itself!"

Happy birthday, Cleveland.

About the Author

Robert K. Rich's true love, besides his family, was storytelling. After retiring from business he combined his sales talent and storytelling ability to become one of the most popular adult education instructors at Cuyahoga Community College, where he taught a variety of history classes. In 1995, as Cleveland's bicentennial approached, he conceived of a series of short essays on Cleveland history. His stories were broadcast regularly on WCPN FM radio and printed as a series in The Plain Dealer leading up to the city's official bicentennial celebration in July 1996.

Born in Pittsburgh, Rich attended the University of Pittsburgh and majored in Engineering. After a brief stint in news media, he had a successful career in sales, primarily in the furniture industry. Mr. Rich loved politics and history and was very involved with Common Cause, a citizen's lobbyist group. An avid tennis player, he hosted a weekly "insecurity council" after his regular game to discuss world affairs. He wryly noted that most people seek fame and fortune and that at least he had his moment of fame. Mr. Rich passed away in 2002.

OTHER BOOKS OF INTEREST . . .

Cleveland's Greatest Disasters!
Sixteen Tragic Tales of Death and Destruction--An Anthology

John Stark Bellamy II

An anthology of the 15 best true Cleveland disaster stories from Bellamy's popular book series, including the apocalyptic East Ohio Gas Company explosion of 1944, the unspeakably horrible 1908 Collinwood School fire, the Ashtabula Bridge Disaster, and the oddly named yet quite ghastly Doodlebug Disaster. Includes 65 photos.

The Top 20 Moments in Cleveland Sports
Tremendous Tales of Heroes and Heartbreaks

Bob Dyer

Relive the most memorable and sensational events in Cleveland sports history. Many of them are known by shorthand: Red Right 88. The Drive. The Fumble. The Shot. Beer Night. Some were gut-wrenching. Some, like the 1964 NFL championship game, were glorious. All are highlight of the shared experience of all Cleveland sports fans.

"Documents what it means to be a Cleveland sports fan: the suffering, the joy and the hope that there is always next year . . . perfect for die-hard Cleveland fans (and really, is there any other kind?)" – News Leader

Gimme Rewrite, Sweetheart
Tales From the Last Glory Days of Cleveland Newspapers—Told By The Men and Women Who Reported the News

John H. Tidyman

Listen in as dozens of veteran newspaper reporters, editors, and photographers swap favorite tales about life on the job at Cleveland's newspapers in the 1950s, '60s, and '70s—when fierce competition made daily newspapers the most exciting business in town. Funny, tragic, sometimes outrageous, it's a boisterous look at "the first draft of history."

"Utterly fascinating . . . highly recommended anyone curious about heyday of newspapers." – Library Book Watch

Read samples at **www.grayco.com**

OTHER BOOKS OF INTEREST . . .

Cleveland TV Tales
Stories from the Golden Age of Local Television

Mike Olszewski, Janice Olszewski

Remember when TV was just three channels and the biggest celebrities in Cleveland were a movie host named Ghoulardi, an elf named Barnaby, and a newscaster named Dorothy Fuldheim? Revisit the early days in these lively stories about the pioneering entertainers who invented television programming before our very eyes. Filled with fun details.

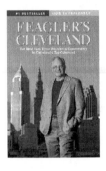

Feagler's Cleveland
The Best from Three Decades of Commentary by Cleveland's Top Columnist

Dick Feagler

Dick Feagler's sharp-witted newspaper columns and TV commentaries defined Cleveland for a generation. Here's a collection of the award-winning columnist's compelling writing about his hometown: 104 essays covering Cleveland politics, sports, crime, people (famous, infamous, and ordinary), and timeless tough issues.

"Feagler has been entertaining, chastising and instructing us for three decades with his newspaper columns. He is our Royko, our Damon Runyan, our Balzac, capturing our foibles and the goofy logic with which we pursue our grand schemes." – Northern Ohio Live

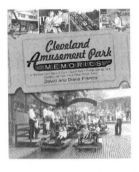

Cleveland Amusement Park Memories
A Nostalgic Look Back at Euclid Beach Park, Puritas Springs Park, Geauga Lake Park, and Other Classic Parks

David & Diane Francis

Northeast Ohioans who grew up visiting amusement parks in the 1940s through 1970s will cherish the memories and memorabilia captured in this vivid, nostalgic portrait of days gone by. Includes: Euclid Beach Park, Luna Park, Geauga Lake Park, Puritas Springs Park, White City, Memphis Kiddie Park, Geneva-on-the-Lake, and others.

Read samples at **www.grayco.com**

Made in the USA
Charleston, SC
17 September 2015